BACKPACKER

THE OUTDOORS AT YOUR DOORSTEP

Day Hiker's Handbook

D0037143

BACKPACKER
THE OUTDOORS AT YOUR DOORSTEP

Day Hiker's Handbook

GET STARTED WITH THE EXPERTS

Michael Lanza

THE MOUNTAINEERS BOOKS

Published by
The Mountaineers Books
1001 SW Klickitat Way, Suite 201
Seattle, WA 98134

33 East Minor Street
Emmaus, PA 18098

First printing 2003, second printing 2005

Published simultaneously in Great Britain by Cordee, 3a DeMontfort Street, Leicester, England, LE1 7HD

Manufactured in the United States of America

Project Editor: Kathleen Cubley
Copyeditor: Dottie Martin
Cover and Book Design: The Mountaineers Books
Layout: Jennifer LaRock Shontz
Illustrator: Jennifer LaRock Shontz
All photographs by the author unless otherwise noted.

Cover photograph: © Rob Bossi
Frontispiece: *A hiker enjoys the view of New Hampshire's White Mountains from atop Mount Bond.*

Library of Congress Cataloging-in-Publication Data
Lanza, Michael A. Lanza, 1961-
   Day hiker's handbook : get started with the experts / Michael Lanza. — 1st ed.
       p. cm.
Includes bibliographical references (p.   ) and index.
   ISBN 0-89886-901-3 (pbk.)
1. Hiking—Handbooks, manuals, etc. I. Title.
GV199.5 .L35 2003
796.51—dc21
                                                2002154577

Contents

Preface

I'm going to hazard a wild guess here and speculate that you've been walking for a lot of years. Odds are you're an adult, and you've been bipedal now for, what, 20 years? 30? Maybe 40, 50, 60, 70 years, or more? That's a lot of experience.

Walking is one of the earliest physical skills we learn. We're really quite good at it. A college anthropology professor once told my class, referring to our species, "We're great walkers." He said this with a pride that I found amusing, the way a parent might boast about a child's athletic skills, but he was right. Although most of us will never excel at running, jumping, throwing a ball, or propelling ourselves on a bicycle or skis, virtually all of us, with a little bit of physical training, are capable of walking impressive distances.

So what keeps most of us from walking up a mountain or off into the woods? It's not our feet—it's our heads. As soon as we change the verb from "walking" to "hiking," some of us have visions of severely strenuous activity, rough terrain, breathing difficulties, sore feet, getting cold and wet, and perhaps worst of all, getting lost. To someone unfamiliar with what lies beyond the trailhead parking lot, the woods and mountains can seem like terra incognita.

I'm writing this to tell you that anyone can learn basic day-hiking skills. This book teaches you those skills simply, without requiring years of postgraduate study. Maybe you've done some day hiking but always went with more-experienced partners who made sure you didn't perish from hypothermia or in the jaws of lions, tigers, or bears. Here's a news flash: *You* can become that more-experienced hiker. This may be an unwise thing for an author of a book like this to admit, but day hiking isn't laser eye surgery. All it takes is a fundamental knowledge of where to go, what to bring, and how to get there and back comfortably and safely. Beyond that, it's just walking—and you're already pretty good at that.

Looking for exercise? Nothing comes more naturally than walking, and the health benefits of walking are well documented. If you already walk or run around town for exercise, just think how much you'll enhance your workout by walking up and down a hill. Add the weight of a light pack on your back and you'll burn even more calories. But a day hike doesn't have to turn into a life-threatening epic on par with climbing Mount Everest, either. If you read this book, yours won't be. Instead, you'll learn how to prepare for and choose the right hike for your abilities, fitness level, and interests.

Of course, hiking isn't all about exercise—that's just a side benefit. Hiking in the forests and mountains is as far removed from hitting your local gym as Kathmandu is from Chicago. Hiking is about walking amid a New England forest ablaze in a kaleidoscope of autumn colors or a vast grove of Rocky Mountain aspen trees turned golden with their own foliage transformation. Hiking takes you to the summits of mountains where you hear and feel the wind and gaze out over a rolling sea of peaks that rearranges your whole idea of the scale of the world. Hiking can take you to the bottom of deep canyons amid colorful stratified rock that harks back nearly to the planet's birth, or it can take you along a rocky seashore where waves pound the land incessantly and seals frolic in the water just offshore. Even if hiking takes you no farther afield than the trails through your local woods, you'll still discover a depth of quiet and peacefulness that you'll wonder how you ever lived without.

Now I'm going to make you a promise: Hiking can transform your life. No, I don't mean you'll suddenly decide to shed your worldly possessions and all of your clothes and go off to live in a cave in the woods. What I do mean is that hiking can change your priorities and perspective on what's important. I speak from experience. Although some avid hikers began as children, I only took it up in my 20s. I was an adult before I discovered the pleasures of hiking, and the activity completely changed my interests and how I spend a big part of my leisure time. It eventually inspired me to redirect my career so that I could make a living from writing about hiking. You may never go that far, but just maybe you'll wish you could.

So read on and enjoy. This book is entertaining as well as informative. But more importantly, transfer what you learn here to the trail. You'll be glad you did.

Michael Lanza

A Note About Safety

Safety is an important concern in all outdoor activities. No book can alert you to every hazard or anticipate the limitations of every reader. The descriptions of techniques and procedures in this book are intended to provide general information. When you follow any of the procedures described here, you assume responsibility for your own safety. Use this book as a general guide to further information. Under normal conditions, excursions into the backcountry require attention to traffic, road and trail conditions, weather, terrain, the capabilities of your party, and other factors. Keeping informed on current conditions and exercising common sense are the keys to a safe, enjoyable outing.

The Mountaineers Books

Introduction

Leave No Trace

Even the most novice of hikers has heard the phrase, "Leave no trace." Most of us have at some time also come across slogans like, "Give a hoot, don't pollute," "Tread lightly," and "Take only pictures, leave only footprints."

Our familiarity with the "leave no trace" message owes to the same effort as does the fact that much of the American backcountry suffers considerably less visible abuse from human use than it did up until the late 1970s and 1980s. That effort, chartered in 1991, consists of the Leave No Trace educational program and guidelines put together by a joint partnership of the National Outdoor Leadership School (NOLS) in Lander, Wyoming; U.S. Forest Service; Bureau of Land Management; National Park Service; and U.S. Fish and Wildlife Service. NOLS administers the program and spearheads the educational effort through a nonprofit organization that also carries the name Leave No Trace, Inc. Leave No Trace, or LNT, consists of seven basic principles, along with a standard curriculum for land managers and educators. Anyone who goes hiking today without seeing discarded candy wrappers, unsightly fire rings, improperly dug cat holes (see Chapter 7 for an explanation of that term and how to go to the bathroom outside), or backpackers washing pots and pans in a lake or leaving a water-runoff trench around their tent has reaped the benefits of this ethic and effort.

To keep our most-cherished places beautiful, we must all contribute to the responsible stewardship of the land. The LNT principles set general guidelines for minimizing our physical impact on the fragile environments where we hike. These guidelines leave some room for interpretation and judgment because it's impossible to create specific rules for every possible situation one can encounter in the backcountry. Besides spelling out those principles here, I've elaborated with some common ways to adhere to them. (For more information about LNT, see Appendix A.)

LNT Principles

1. Plan ahead and prepare.
2. Travel and camp on durable surfaces.

3. Dispose of waste properly.
4. Leave what you find.
5. Minimize campfire impacts.
6. Respect wildlife.
7. Be considerate of other visitors.

How does a conscientious hiker translate these guidelines to his or her own behavior? First, simply recall the principles, not necessarily memorize them, but think about what they mean and how to use them when you're on the trail. In addition, pack out all trash—period—even biodegradable items like orange and banana peels. If the food waste isn't native to the environment you're in, it doesn't belong there. Trash attracts scavengers, many of which chase away native species and begin to associate people with food. For example, Australia has experienced an incredible increase in rat populations in recreational areas because too many people are chucking trash trailside. Carry a zipper-lock bag in your pocket, and fill it with garbage you find along the trail—you'll do a world of good and teach a child a good lesson.

Follow the designated main trail and avoid shortcuts. Wear gaiters and walk through the mud rather than going around puddles or soft sections of the trail, which widens trails. Walk on durable surfaces such as gravel, sand, rock, snow, dry alpine meadows, and grasslands. When in a group, walk single file on trails but spread out when hiking cross-country.

Backpackers who camp in the backcountry should follow the land managers' guidelines for camping. If there aren't regulations, your first choice should be a well-established site, where ground vegetation is worn away, but decomposing leaves and needles are still present in spots. Don't camp in sites where prior use is only slightly noticeable (that is, flattened grass and leaves, scattered charcoal). If there are no well-established sites, camp in a spot that shows no signs of prior use. Never rearrange the landscape to suit your needs. Camp out of view of the main trail and at least 200 feet from water sources.

Second, take a look at what your sole does to the ground. On a packed-dirt trail, chances are you can't even find your boot track. However, on wet trails or tundra, or off-trail, every step can leave an unsightly gash. In those places, step on rocks, tough vegetation, firm soil, and snow. If you see an unmarked, bare-dirt trail, use it; otherwise try not to walk where other people have stepped. Avoid cutting into sidehills; if your treads expose fresh dirt, seek tougher ground. Be even more careful along streambanks and in other erosion-prone areas. Treat footfalls as what they are: blows to the earth that can leave a bruise or even an open wound.

Finally, but perhaps most importantly, support local hiking clubs and organizations that maintain trails and volunteer for trail work and campsite monitoring projects. See Appendix A for a partial list of such groups.

Stick to the trail rather than walking on delicate wildflowers such as these diapensia blooming on New Hampshire's Mount Washington.

One Last Thing . . .

As you become a seasoned hiker, you'll come to recognize and appreciate the hard labor that goes into maintaining thousands and thousands of miles of trails across the country. Much of that work, even on public lands, is done by volunteer trail maintenance crews and nonprofit conservation organizations and hiking clubs such as those listed in Appendix A. These organizations do good work and are always in need of support, both in the form of money and volunteer hours. Join the organization in your area; support the group that maintains your favorite hiking destination. Help in any way you can—it's almost as satisfying as hiking.

We're interested in your feedback about this book's content and presentation so that we can improve it for future editions. Send your comments to The Mountaineers Books, 1001 Southwest Klickitat Way, Suite 201, Seattle, WA 98134. Visit The Mountaineers Books' website at *www.mountaineersbooks.org* or *Backpacker* magazine's website at *www.backpacker.com*.

Chapter 1

Getting Started

Where do I start? Good question, right? To the person who decides to try hiking, taking that "first step," so to speak, can seem as alien as traveling to another planet. Where do I go? How do I find places to hike? What do I need? Will I be able to find my way? Is it unsafe? What's out there?

Those are all good, legitimate questions. Fortunately, the answers are easy. Wherever you live in this country, there is a place nearby where you can hike. It may be a city or state park or forest; a conservation area open to the public; or a national park, forest, or seashore. Many places may be private land on which the owner allows public access to a trail system. The last two words in that sentence are key here: "trail system." No, you don't absolutely need trails to go hiking, but trails are much easier to walk than thick forest or even open terrain where footing can be uncertain—and, of course, trails make finding your way much easier. You may be surprised by how many trails are near your home, how easy they are to reach, how pleasant they are to walk, and how many other people are out there hiking, running, bird watching, and taking their kids for a walk.

How do you find these places? Let your fingers do the walking before your feet do. The telephone book lists your area's recreation department and state parks and recreation department. Call them for information; they often have maps and literature available for free (or a nominal fee) that can be mailed to your home or picked up at their office or various outlets in your community (for example, retail

Most day hikes are on easy trails, often with spectacular views such as this one from Maine's Cadillac Mountain in Acadia National Park.

stores that sell hiking and camping gear). Visit your local outdoor gear retailer and ask employees where to find information about hiking locally and around your region. They probably have shelves of guidebooks and maps to help you. Ask them whether there's a local or regional hiking club or conservation organization that holds organized hikes. Search the World Wide Web for information about hiking destinations and clubs in your area.

City, state, and national public lands have extensive systems of marked trails for hikers. If you live in a populous area, you'll find there are a lot of other people just like you out day-hiking the area's most accessible trails—men, women, and children of all ages who are friendly and helpful. You will hardly feel isolated or too far removed from civilization. Many of these trails have signs that show the way.

You also start hiking by demystifying the experience and realizing it's something you can do today, right now, before you read any further into this book. That's right. There are many "hikes" out there that are simply straightforward "walks" that happen to follow a trail instead of a sidewalk. So find a local city or state park or state forest or conservation area with a well-marked, easy-to-follow trail system; grab a map of the place (often available for free at the park or forest office or posted at trail junctions); ask someone in the know at the park to help you determine the distance and difficulty of specific trails; and go for a walk for an hour or two or three. The experience will make you feel great physically, give you a little boost of confidence, and help you understand that hiking takes many forms.

The easiest hikes out there don't really demand all that much in the way of preparation or training, so there's no reason to postpone your baptismal dip into the wonderful adventure that is hiking. In fact, your hiking "education" will be better furthered if you regularly take what you've read in the pages and chapters that follow and apply that knowledge to hikes that are within your evolving abilities. The goal of this book is to help you progress as far as you want to beyond those

easy, well-marked state park trails and to give you the skills and confidence to hike wherever your wanderlust leads you.

If you've already done some day hiking, you probably understand that some hikes are much more accessible than others by virtue of having a good footpath that's easy to follow and find your way along. Those are good hikes with which to begin. There's really little risk of getting "lost," and even a moment of uncertainty about where exactly you are, or a wrong turn, isn't likely to get you into trouble— you'll probably figure out soon enough that you're not too far off course and correct your direction. Furthermore, local parks with well-maintained trail systems that remain in the woods simply don't pose the potential risks and problems that can crop up when hiking more rugged trails in mountains. These easier hikes provide a nice introduction to reading a trail map—which in this type of situation you'll find no more challenging than reading a road map. In a way, learning day-hiking skills is a little bit like learning to walk: In the beginning, how far and where you'll go is limited; but as you get better, you find yourself able to explore farther afield—and it becomes more fun.

Some trails are on challenging terrain, such as Mount Adams' summit in New Hampshire's Presidential Range.

Finding Hiking Partners

As you begin, you may feel safer and surer of yourself if accompanied by hiking partners who have similar goals as you and perhaps a little more experience. Hiking will also be more enjoyable if you're not anxious about making a big mistake or wondering whether you've gotten yourself in over your head.

Finding such partners can seem like the first big obstacle to hiking, but often, potential partners are all around—you only have to start looking. Talk about hiking with family, friends, co-workers, people you know through civic groups or activities, or the person working in the store where you buy your outdoor gear. You'll be surprised at how many people—and sometimes *which* people—share your interest or know someone who does. In fact, I've always found that wherever I go and wherever I live, there are more potential hiking partners than I could ever want. Finding partners becomes more a matter of talking to people about the kind of hiking they prefer and making sure the people I ultimately hit the trail with have the same idea of what I consider "hiking"—but more on that soon.

There are hiking clubs and conservation organizations in virtually every corner of the country, and most of them conduct regular, organized group hikes for members. They also often devote tremendous resources to preserving the places we all like to hike, which makes their cause worthy of our financial and other support. You'll find these local and regional organizations, or chapters of national organizations, in every major city and in every state. Look for them through local outdoor gear retailers, in outdoor magazines, and on websites of major conservation organizations where local chapter leaders are listed. In addition, see Appendix A for a listing of hiking clubs and conservation organizations around the country. Members are typically people just like you who've joined to learn more about outdoor activities such as hiking, find like-minded people to do those things with, and perhaps support the organization's conservation and trail-maintenance programs. Many members are often novices, so some day hikes are specifically for beginners.

The hikes are often led by volunteer trip leaders who have a good deal of hiking and backcountry experience and are capable of ensuring the comfort, enjoyment, and safety of the group—as much as that can be ensured, given that no one can anticipate accidents such as a sprained ankle. These organized hikes are a great way to meet other hikers and to learn the skills for heading off into the mountains and forests on your own.

Being a Smart Consumer

Before signing up for an organized hike, call the trip leader and ask the following pertinent questions about the type of hike it is:

- ▲ How long will it be in miles?
- ▲ What's the estimated time it will take to complete the hike, and what will the pace be like?

- ▲ What's the experience and fitness level required of participants?
- ▲ How rough is the trail?
- ▲ How much elevation gain and loss will there be over the course of the hike?
- ▲ What's the weather expected to be like?

In addition, ask about the experience level of the trip leaders; you should feel confident of their ability as well as your own.

Find out as much as possible about the hike before signing up for it. Sometimes beginners let a trip leader take care of all the planning, trusting that person to make the correct decisions. Although it makes sense to rely on the leader's judgment in some situations, that person cannot know your expectations for the hike.

I'll illustrate my point with an anecdote that involves skiing instead of hiking. Some years ago, I hiked into Tuckerman Ravine on Mount Washington, in New Hampshire's White Mountain National Forest, to write a story about the enormous popularity of spring skiing the ravine's very steep headwall. It's quite a sight and worth going to watch if you're in that area between roughly late March and late May to mid-June, when the snow usually melts. It's also a beautiful hike anytime but especially on a sunny, warm spring day when snow and ice still cling to the cliffs of Tuckerman. Hundreds of people head up the hiking trail (the snow melts off the trail at lower elevations long before it melts off the ravine headwall) carrying skis, rubber tubes, plastic sleds, and all manner of conveyance for sliding on snow.

In the ravine, at the base of the daunting headwall, those with courage and confidence kick steps slowly up the headwall—which grows increasingly steeper the higher you go—until they reach a point they feel is not too steep for them to ski down. However, some who've gone with friends who are superior skiers have found themselves in terrain steeper than anything they've ever skied before, but they're reluctant to admit this to themselves or their compadres. (Young men are particularly prone to this dangerous condition in which the ego eclipses one's judgment.)

On this particular day, I sat in the warm sun in an area called Lunch Rocks with volunteer ski patrollers who hang out in the ravine on spring weekends just in case someone gets hurt. As we talked, one of them pointed out a group of four young men who had climbed up nearly to the top of the headwall and were now putting on their skis and lining up to ski down. "Watch," one ski patroller told me. "The first skiers to go down will do fine. The last one will fall and slide all the way to the bottom." His prediction proved true, as the last skier in this group failed to execute more than one turn and rode his ski pants to the ravine floor—fortunately, without getting hurt. It often happens that way, this ski patroller explained to me. Skiers of modest ability are convinced to try to ski Tuckerman by friends who are better skiers. The better skiers always go first, as if a pecking order of skill was preestablished. The last skiers are almost invariably the worst in the group and often lack the skills to ski the steep headwall.

You may never attempt something as challenging or risky as skiing a mountain ravine headwall, but there are parallels between hiking and my tale of Tuckerman tumbles. It's important that everyone who intends to participate in a group hike be aware of the plan and understand what's involved to avoid the discomfort or worse that can happen when different people have greatly contrasting visions of the day's plans or when someone isn't prepared in terms of equipment, ability, physical condition, or mental readiness. (Remember this rule when the time comes that you're the hike leader organizing less-experienced people who may be inclined to not ask questions and simply let you make all the decisions.) Even someone who is very fit may not be psychologically comfortable with certain kinds of difficult terrain that may be encountered on a hike; that person can drastically slow down the rest of the group, which then threatens to cause other potential problems, such as the group not finishing the hike before dark. For this reason, many trip leaders are actually trained to have the type of conversation I'm suggesting with everyone who inquires about joining the hike. In addition, a club magazine or newsletter listing organized hikes will indicate the difficulty level and experience and fitness levels expected of participants.

Remember that you're considering signing up for an itinerary that's already set, and barring unexpected bad weather or other problems, the others in the group will likely expect everyone on the hike to be able to complete it. If the hike sounds much harder than you've ever done, or like you're biting off more than you can chew, look for another one. Trust your intuition in judging whether a particular hike is appropriate for you. These organizations typically schedule numerous hikes every month; they'll have one that fits your abilities and interests.

Doing It Yourself

You may be ready to cobble together your own group of friends for a hike of your own choosing, or maybe signing up for an organized group hike with people you don't know just isn't your thing. Nonetheless, you now know the importance of selecting a hike that's appropriate to your experience, fitness level, abilities, and interests—and those of your companions. Take that same approach as you plan a hike yourself.

"How hard will that hike be? How long will it take?" Those two questions ask a lot, and the answers depend as much on the hikers as on the nature of the hike itself. Finding the right hike for yourself and your companions comes down to assessing the hike itself as well as the physical condition and emotional comfort level of the hikers—remembering that a group's pace and goals should and will be dictated by the slowest person.

Consider the hikers in the following three scenarios (their names have been changed to protect the innocent):

Scenario 1: Cher is somewhere past age 50 (she doesn't like to disclose her age), willing to try new things, and relatively fit, thanks to a regular exercise regimen that gets her out fitness walking or to the gym 4 to 5 days a week. She doesn't have any problems with her knees or other chronic injuries. She's hiked some well-maintained, wide, easy-to-follow trails in the local state park, covering up to about 8 miles in numerous half-day outings on those trails. However, she's never hiked a trail up a mountain, where she might encounter rougher, rockier trails; a lot more uphill and downhill; and possibly some terrain above tree line that's exposed to wind and weather.

Where to start: Cher's ready to tackle a small mountain of moderate difficulty. She should choose a place that's popular, which usually translates to having good, well-marked, albeit rocky trails and the help of other hikers should she need it. She would probably find that a hike of 6 to 8 miles round trip that climbs about 1500 to 2500 feet in elevation presents a challenge that takes several hours but lies within her abilities. If her first summit is more than about 8000 feet above sea level, however, she should first skip ahead in this chapter to the section about moderating your goals at higher elevations.

Scenario 2: Elvis is in his 30s and has let himself go in recent years, rarely exercising and putting on some padding around his waist as a result of working long hours and traveling a lot for his job. Still, he wants to take up hiking as a fun way to get back in shape, and he's serious about it. He's even gotten his doctor's advice on starting an exercise program. He wants to start hiking soon, and he realizes he should ease into this new activity.

Where to start: Elvis sounds like he's well on the way to getting his health back on track and enjoying himself, but he's wise to take things slowly. He should look for hikes that are described as easy in guidebooks or by land managers and that are on well-marked trails, offer good footing, and don't have many hills. Assuming that—aside from being a bit overweight—his health is otherwise good, Elvis might try a relatively flat hike of a couple of miles to start with and see how he feels afterward. As he gains strength and stamina, he can gradually increase his distance.

Scenario 3: Madonna is in her early 30s and has been a fitness fanatic since college. She's buff. She rarely misses a workout in the gym, and depending on the season, she regularly runs, bicycles, or cross-country skis and has entered citizen races in all three sports. She's done several day hikes of smaller mountains and regularly runs trails in the local city park. She's eager to get more into hiking, her new favorite activity.

Where to start: Madonna is ready physically and probably mentally for a difficult day hike, but she's still a novice at the broader skills required for long, committing hikes in the mountains. She should find some more-experienced hikers who share her passion for fitness and athletic challenge who can take her on difficult hikes, where finding one's way and dealing with variables such as weather become more complicated. They can take her on all-day hikes involving 10 miles or more

Every hiker should learn basic map-reading skills, as this hiker does in Idaho's Sawtooth National Recreation Area.

and 3000 feet or more of up and down, and possibly rough terrain, which she'll likely find challenging yet fun. All the while, she'll glean valuable skills that will help her take such hikes without her friends' guidance soon enough.

How Hard Is *Hard*?

After deciding what you and your companions are ready for, take some measure of the factors that determine the relative difficulty of any hike you're considering. In all likelihood, you have plenty of information readily available to help you determine that. You probably know of the hike because of a guidebook—which should offer a difficulty rating or describe the hike enough to get a sense of that—or through someone who can tell you about the hike. Hiking clubs, employees at outdoor gear stores, land managers, and the World Wide Web are all good sources for information about a hike's difficulty. They sometimes offer different or contradictory information, so the more sources you tap for information, the better prepared you'll be to interpret it. Their perspective on what's "hard" may also differ significantly from your own, so consider the source when you evaluate any information or recommendations you receive.

Several factors affect a hike's relative difficulty. Most obvious is the distance, which requires no explanation and may be the first question you ask; however, distance is just one part of a big equation.

How much elevation does the hike gain and lose over its course? Going uphill is fatiguing, especially on a rocky trail, but going downhill can sometimes seem harder because of the stresses it places on certain muscles and joints. Novice hikers in decent physical condition may find 1000 to 2000 feet of elevation gain quite hard, although seasoned hikers might easily dispatch 4000 to 5000 feet, or much more, of elevation in a day.

On a good trail, a common formula used to calculate the length of time required to complete a hike is to assume a pace of 2 miles per hour (mph), plus another hour for every 1000 feet of uphill hiking. Extrapolating from that, one might figure each 1000 feet of climbing to make an equivalent demand on your energy level of 2 relatively flat trail miles—but that's assuming a good trail. Most important is to know your limitations.

As mentioned in Scenario 1 involving Cher, many popular hikes—though certainly not all—tend to follow trails with good footing where you're not likely to get lost. When calculating a hike's difficulty, weigh the ruggedness of the trail. How nimbly you move on a rugged, rocky trail varies depending on how many such trails you've hiked and your psychological comfort level on them. Most hikers are slowed on a rocky trail; some are slowed significantly. Unless you know from experience that you (and your companions) move quickly on such a trail, expect rugged trails to lengthen your hiking time. Similarly, although popular trails are often wide, well-marked paths that are easy to follow, less-popular trails, especially those that are more remote, may be overgrown, not well marked, and very hard to follow—which will certainly slow you down (see Chapter 6). Again, find out what you can about a trail beforehand.

As mentioned earlier, the elevation above sea level comes into play in some mountains of the western United States. In general, most people start to feel some shortness of breath and greater fatigue between 8000 and 10,000 feet above sea level. If you live at sea level and plan to hike in the mountains above 8000 or 10,000 feet—especially if you plan to attempt a summit above 12,000 or 14,000 feet, which are numerous in some western states—you might come down with a mild case of acute mountain sickness (AMS). AMS consists of a worsening headache and upset stomach. Everyone reacts differently to altitude, and your tolerance for it does not improve if you are in good shape. The best prevention is to take as much time as you can afford to acclimate to gradually higher elevations. For example, if you want to hike a Colorado **fourteener** (what hikers call Colorado's fifty-four summits that are more than 14,000 feet), spend a night or three sleeping in town before the hike—many mountain towns sit between 7000 and 10,000 feet—and do short **acclimation hikes** to 10,000 or 12,000 feet before your big hike. You can also sleep at elevation and do acclimation hikes on weekends before your big hike, if your schedule permits. Hike slowly at high elevations, striving always to maintain an easy, steady rhythm to your breathing; don't push so hard that your breathing is labored. Also, maintaining proper hydration becomes critical the higher you go, so drink a lot of fluids and eat as much as you can to maintain your energy level. Finally, the cure for AMS is to turn around and go downhill; don't wait until you (or a companion) feel too ill to walk down. You'll often feel better as soon as you get to a lower elevation.

This table offers some examples of how the difficulty of a hike and how long it takes can vary widely depending on the hikers and other variables.

Estimating Hiking Time

Variable	Party 1	Party 2
	Fit pair of experienced hikers, both age 30, who've done this hike numerous times and done many hikes of much greater difficulty in all kinds of weather	Same fit pair from Party 1, along with the parents of one of the experienced hikers— a reasonably fit couple in their 50s who hike only occasionally
Normal conditions	Total hiking time = 4 hrs	Total hiking time = 6.5 hrs
Final mile of trail before summit is rocky, making footing difficult	Total hiking time = 4.5 hrs	Total hiking time = 7.5 hrs
Rain begins at summit, making rocks on upper trail wet on descent	Total hiking time = 4.75 hrs	Total hiking time = 8 hrs
Hike began at midday in early fall, when days are shorter, so darkness occurs within 2 miles of the trail's end	Total hiking time = 5 hrs	Total hiking time = 8.5 hrs

A well-maintained, well-marked trail with solid footing to the summit of a 4000-foot mountain on a dry, comfortably warm day, ascending 2000 feet and hiking 7 miles round trip. Both parties spend 30 minutes enjoying the view at the summit.

How to Decipher a Hike Description

A good hike description provides all the information needed to choose a hike appropriate to your interests and abilities.

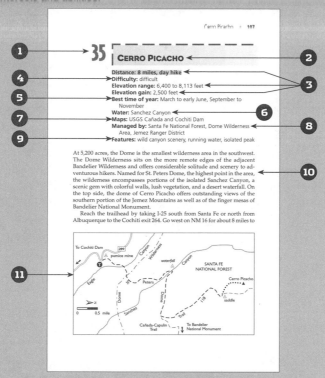

1 The hike's **number** corresponds with a number on the hike locator map, which shows the general location for all hikes in the book.

2 The hike's **name** identifies the peak, trail, park, or other key landmark.

3 The hike's **distance, maximum elevation,** and **total elevation gained** provide important specific indicators of the hike's difficulty.

4 The hike's **difficulty** indicates how challenging the hike will be (check each book's Introduction to see how difficulty levels are defined).

5 The **season** or **recommended months** describe the best time to hike an area, which may depend on elevation and climate.

6 The **water** information indicates where to find water sources during the hike.

7 The **maps** covering the hike are named (for example, "USGS Cañada and Cochiti Dam" are the names of two USGS quad maps).

8 The **management agency** indicates what agency maintains the hike area. Management agencies are additional sources for information regarding the hike or other features in surrounding areas.

9 The hike's **features** summarize highlights of the hike.

10 The hike's **description** provides driving directions to the trailhead and more detail of the hike's natural attractions, along with specifics of the hiking route itself.

11 The hike's **map** illustrates the general layout of the hike; however, always bring a more detailed map, such as one published by the U.S. Geological Survey or U.S. Forest Service.

Page excerpted from *100 Hikes in™ New Mexico*, 2nd Edition by Craig Martin.

Keeping Your Engine Tuned

Whether you're a hiker or snowboarder or elite mountaineer, or whatever you do, you'll enjoy yourself more, and be less prone to injury, if you keep in shape. However, you don't have to do double-session daily workouts at the U.S. Olympic Training Center to prepare for weekend day hikes. At a recreational level of activity, most injuries related to hiking (and other sports) occur at least in part because of inadequate physical conditioning: You get tired near the end of a hike and are more likely to trip and fall or to strain a muscle or tendon because you didn't stretch it adequately before beginning your hike. Those injuries, fortunately, are largely avoidable.

It doesn't take much effort or time to get in shape, and you're probably already doing at least something. Maintain an exercise program of three or four cardio-vascular workouts a week of at least 30 minutes each. These should be intense workouts that elevate your heart rate to around 80 percent of its maximum rate for your age. Optimally, each week you'll also have at least one workout (or hike) that's twice as long as your daily workouts or longer. This doesn't require a high-priced trainer, but if you belong to a health club you could see whether it offers a program. If you prefer a personalized program, develop with a personal trainer a tailor-made training regimen to prepare for a season of hiking. Walking regularly is great training for most easy to moderately difficult hikes. Training programs are described in *Backpacker* magazine, and you'll find good advice in *Conditioning for Outdoor Fitness* (The Mountaineers Books, 1999).

I'm a devotee of regular stretching. To prevent injury and reduce or prevent the soreness and stiffness that sometimes follows a hard hike or workout, stretch for 10 or 15 minutes before and after activity. This book isn't intended to be a comprehensive stretching guide; that information is widely available in other books and at the local gym. Find exercises that stretch the major muscles, including calves, quadriceps, hamstrings, buttocks, neck, back, and shoulders. Regular abdominal exercises such as crunches, even for a few minutes a day or a few times a week, help protect you from lower-back injury (but make sure you do them correctly).

Nothing gets your body ready for hiking better than hiking. Hit the local trails after work or on the weekends. If you haven't hiked since last season, start out with modest distances without a pack (assuming you don't need a pack on these "training hikes") or with a light pack, and gradually increase the weight and distance on subsequent hikes. Even if you were in great hiking shape last season, your body may not necessarily be ready for the stresses of long hikes with a heavy pack. Work up to those. Hike hills if you have access to them, use stair-climbing equipment at the gym, hike flights of stairs in your office building, or do sets of step-ups at home. Some hiking clubs also offer training tips and programs.

If you're taking up physical activity after a long period—weeks, months, or years—of relative inactivity, ease yourself into an exercise or hiking program and get your doctor's advice before starting. Find an activity you like that is convenient

Stretching before and after a hike helps prevent stiffness and injury.

to do regularly and provides an aerobic and muscular workout, whether it's running, cycling, fitness walking, or going to the gym. Don't overdue it at the outset; that's a prescription for injury.

The older you are, the more prone you are to injury resulting from overexerting before your body is ready for it. As we age, stretching and maintaining muscle tone and flexibility becomes more important to avoiding injury. Age is not a barrier to being active; it's merely a hurdle to clear—and before jumping, make sure you know what's on the other side. That is, take it slowly and get some advice from a professional, whether it be a doctor, physical therapist, or someone at your health club who works with "older athletes."

If someone tells you that hiking will never hurt, you tell that person I said that's a lot of horse hooey. Although it varies with the difficulty and amount of hiking you do, the truth is that this sport can be hard on your body, just as with any physical activity. You might get sore muscles and knees, hurt your ankles or feet, or get a sore back from carrying a pack. I've endured my share of those aches and pains. Nevertheless, I still hike because it sure beats lying around on the couch, taking inventory of what hurts. Hiking is a much more benign activity than many others we do. You can avoid most injuries—whether from hiking or any other physical activity—simply by adhering to a regular program of exercise and stretching.

Hiking in Groups

Hiking is a very social activity, and hiking with a big group of family or friends is one of the most enjoyable things I can think of doing. Yet, I can also recall numerous times I've encountered large groups of strangers on the trail whose behavior demonstrated a lack of consideration for me and other hikers: conversing loudly and obnoxiously; talking loudly into cellular phones; and—believe it or not—playing a boom box at high volume. (Why someone would carry such a thing up a mountain far exceeds my ability to explain here.) When we hike in groups, we have a responsibility to be considerate of other hikers. For instance, although our inclination may be to talk and laugh, others may be out there for the peacefulness and quietude, and we should always respect that. If we don't adhere to an ethic of consideration for others on the trail, we'll ultimately suffer the consequences when the day comes that *we're* on a quiet hike and run into a loud, disrespectful group.

Keep the following guidelines in mind:

▲ On some public lands, regulations limit group size to ten people. Know and follow any such rules.

▲ Regardless of whether there are rules, if you have a large group, spread out along the trail to minimize your noise and conspicuousness.

▲ Keep conversations at a moderate level and keep children under a modest level of control.

▲ Step aside and yield the trail to hikers coming in the other direction. Be aware of hikers behind you who may want to pass your group, and step aside for them.

▲ Choose an appropriate destination for the group. Popular hikes that attract many people are not places that hikers go to seek quiet and solitude anyway, therefore they're perfect for groups, especially children. If you're not sure where to take such a group, call the land managers; they usually have suggestions.

Hiking Alone

I've hiked and backpacked solo in all four seasons, on popular trails and in remote wilderness areas, and had some of my most rewarding—and sometimes my most difficult—experiences in the backcountry. The sense of solitude and quiet you'll discover on a trail with no other people around is something you'll never achieve even with just one companion in a remote place. The challenge for the person who's prepared for a solo hike can foster a powerful feeling of confidence and accomplishment. I'll certainly hike alone again and expect to do so for many years to come.

Wait—isn't hiking alone unsafe? Well, yes and no. There's an old hiking maxim that says you should never hike alone. Without question, it is good advice for novice hikers. However, hiking solo is not inherently unsafe or unwise—it is simply less safe than hiking with companions. That's an important distinction. Yes, hiking alone is less safe for the obvious reason that if you get hurt while alone, there's no one around to help you. On the other hand, statistically you're probably still at greater risk driving to the trailhead than while hiking alone. Women are, unfortunately, probably at greater risk than men when hiking alone, which is a poor reflection on our society, yet the incidence of violence to women on the trail is still extremely low.

Am I suggesting that you hike alone? No. That's a decision only you can make after carefully and honestly assessing whether you're ready for it. You may never desire to try it, and that's fine. Hiking is not a competition, and it doesn't matter whether you ever hike solo.

Hiking's rewards far outweigh the effort. The reward here is a view of the Colorado River along the Grand Canyon's Tonto Trail.

If you do hike alone, bear this in mind: Your margin for error is greatly reduced when you hike alone, so you should respond to that by significantly lowering the level of risk you consider acceptable. You might read that sentence and think, "But I wouldn't accept any risk at all!" In reality, we accept a certain level of risk in everyday life without thinking about it, every time we get behind the wheel of a car or board a plane or walk a city street, for instance. Certainly, hiking in the woods or mountains, even with companions, invites some amount of risk that varies depending on the terrain, trail condition, weather, season, remoteness, your experience, and other factors. We accept many of these risk levels because either the situation is so familiar that we don't feel we're in great danger—like driving a car—or because we've thought out the situation and feel we're prepared for it, like most of the hikes we take.

Assessing your readiness to hike alone comes down to familiarity with whatever you could encounter. Choose a trail you've done many times or a hike that's popular or easier than many you've done in the past, and you will probably feel no nervousness and little risk. As you ramp up the difficulty level, you increase the risk factor. To reduce that risk factor, make increasingly conservative decisions. Don't venture out above tree line in weather that appears somewhat questionable, even if you'd do it without a second thought if other people were along. Turn back at the stream crossing that looks iffy. Think about how far you are from help and how long it could be before someone is likely to find you if you're injured. You greatly increase your risk when you extend yourself beyond your abilities when alone. Save those challenging hikes for when you have capable companions to join you.

Think about the following things before and during a solo hike:

▲ Be honest with yourself about your physical ability and experience to head out alone on your selected hike.

▲ Depending on the hike, bring extra water, food, and clothing; a cellular phone; and perhaps a sleeping bag and pad in case you're stuck somewhere waiting for help. If you expect cold temperatures and are going out for several miles and hours, all of these things are a must.

▲ Tell someone where you're going and when you plan to return.

Women Hiking Alone

"No way," you might be thinking about the notion of hiking alone as a woman. Unfortunately, we live in a world in which women have to think more seriously about personal safety and security than do men. The rules don't change when you're out amid nature's beauty. The truth is that the nation's trails are statistically safe—crime is virtually unheard of on the trail. Many women safely hike alone. As with men, the greatest risks facing women are those presented by the natural environment along with the risk of making a mistake that leads to trouble. If you feel confident enough in your hiking and outdoor skills that you believe you can hike alone, bring the same wariness of strangers into the woods that you have when walking city streets. Don't assume people you don't know are trustworthy. Carry a whistle but not weapons. Trust your instincts: If unsavory characters appear, move on, don't announce your plans, and if you exchange any words with them, refer to your husband or boyfriend who is coming up the trail. In short, use good judgment—and if in your judgment you'd rather not hike alone, that's fine, too.

Taking Baby Steps

I made the analogy earlier that learning hiking skills is a little like learning to walk. It's a conservative philosophy I've applied to everything I've taken up over the years, from wilderness travel and winter hiking to rock climbing and backcountry skiing. It's a philosophy that places safety and enjoyment above everything else, and it's prompted me on many occasions to turn back and abandon my plans in favor of a safe retreat instead of attempting something that I'm not fully confident I can do.

From one perspective, it probably doesn't sound like a philosophy that the most-daring outdoor enthusiasts would embrace. Elite mountaineers don't get to

Many trails are well-maintained footpaths that offer easy walking, such as this trail to Iceberg Lake in Glacier National Park, Montana.

Some trails are rugged and involve scrambling, but even a physically fit pregnant woman can hike them. Here, a woman pregnant 5 months hikes New Hampshire's Mount Washington.

the summits of the world's highest peaks by always turning back when things start to look grim, right? In reality, they just operate on a different risk scale than most of us. They accept higher risks in pursuit of their goals, sure, but many of them also admit that they've turned back many times when what lay ahead seemed too much for them to attempt on that particular day. As the late, great American climber and lifelong outdoor educator Paul Petzoldt famously said, "There are old climbers, and there are bold climbers, but there are no old, bold climbers."

My conservative philosophy boils down to this maxim: Try new things, yes, but to maximize your safety and comfort, take on new challenges in small increments. You are safest when in familiar situations where you understand what's going on, what can potentially go wrong, and what to do when something does go wrong. You are most at risk when you wander into unfamiliar territory, where you're not entirely sure of your environment and the consequences of your actions. You don't feel endangered in your own home, right? That's because it's an extremely familiar environment and you know how to manage it. Think of hiking in the mountains in the same way—knowing your environment and what can happen is the key to emotional comfort and safety. No sensible person would think a day hike along the seashore in Maine's Acadia National Park is adequate training for climbing Mount Everest. Similarly, approach increasingly more difficult hikes as if you're progressing from one grade level to the next, rather than skipping grades.

Take baby steps. Progress gradually into new challenges. Don't step too far beyond your zone of familiarity. As you gain experience, your zone of familiarity will expand and you'll feel comfortable taking on hikes that at one time may have seemed impossible for you. There's no need or reason to rush into it. As the old saying goes, the mountains will still be there next time.

How does that philosophy translate into decision making on the trail? Again, trust your intuition and think about the abilities and comfort level of everyone in the group, because the slowest member dictates the group's pace. If you have good information about the hike before you even pull on your boots; have a good understanding of what you and your companions are ready for; and stay alert, you'll avoid most problems. However, don't head out on the trail with your itinerary set in stone in your mind and the minds of your hiking mates. Go out realizing you may have to change course according to the whim of variables such as weather or someone in the group starting to feel ill. Know before going out what your options would be to shorten your hike—often it's simply turning back, but that's not always the best option. This advice may seem glaringly obvious, but in fact, many hikers (and climbers, backpackers, and kayakers, etc.) head out with their planned itinerary so firmly set in their minds that the thought of changing their plan doesn't immediately occur to them when the first signs appear suggesting that a change in course would be wise. It's nothing more than a mental exercise, a frame of mind.

Now bear in mind, day hiking ranks far below Himalayan mountaineering on the danger scale. Statistically, you're much more likely to buy that one-way ticket to the great trailhead in the sky while driving to and from your hike than while on the trail (see Chapter 6). Nevertheless, trails are inherently more difficult to walk on than asphalt (and much more pleasant), so hikers occasionally turn ankles, trip, and fall. They occasionally stray too far from their zone of familiarity and get into trouble. Often, the reason for their troubles is simply that they had their mental radar turned off and they weren't paying close attention to what they were doing and where they were. That's when you trip and fall, fail to notice the trail junction you wanted, or not realize a storm is brewing until it's upon you. A fundamental tenet of safe hiking is simply staying on your toes—not literally, of course—but keeping your eyes open. Keep your senses tuned to what's going on around you, and your brain will take care of notifying you when it sees something it doesn't like.

Setting Reasonable Goals

How do you decide what are reasonable goals for yourself? Consider the three scenarios earlier in this chapter concerning our fictional novice hikers: Cher, Elvis, and Madonna. They took up hiking from different places on the continuums of physical fitness, comfort level, and difficulty. In each case, I proposed an immediate strategy for their introduction to hiking—but there's no telling where each will go from those humble roots. Cher may remain perfectly content tackling nothing more difficult than moderate jaunts up popular, small hills and mountains on easy-to-follow trails. Elvis might drop twenty pounds and become a hard-core hiker, backpacker, and wilderness traveler. Madonna might fall in love with the physical aspect of hiking and the athleticism of longer, harder, fast hikes and thus pursue only that type of experience. Any one of them may only hike occasionally, or every weekend; one may stick to hikes close to home, while another explores trails and peaks across the country or world. A world of opportunities and experiences await each of them, one as diverse as virtually any recreational activity they might take up. Whatever route they take, they won't be disappointed.

The plethora of possibilities lying ahead of Cher, Elvis, and Madonna illustrates the impossibility of setting appropriate, specific goals for another person. If a formula existed for calculating that, it might look something like this:

Subject A's Experience Range* + Physical Condition† + Mental State‡ = Appropriate Goal

* Where she's hiked, how far, in what weather, etc.

† Fitness level, how well she's eaten and slept recently, presence of nagging injuries

‡ Comfort level, belief that she can do the hike

The third variable in the equation—her comfort with the hike and whether she believes she can do it—may be the most important factor of all—and only she can know that. People have been known to complete the entire 2158-mile Appalachian Trail with little previous hiking or backpacking experience, driving themselves by force of will and determination. I've also seen people who've hiked and backpacked for years become completely unhinged on a narrow and exposed trail with steep, long drop-offs to either side.

So, you have to determine for yourself what are reasonable goals. That said, apply the philosophy mentioned earlier and think out all the ramifications of ramping up the challenge and of doing more than you've done before. Are you ready to increase your single-day maximum hiking distance and elevation gain by 10 percent, 20 percent, or 50 percent? Are you ready for a considerably more rugged and obscure trail than you've attempted before? Are you with people who can handle any situation you might encounter? How far will you be at any time from the nearest road—and thus, from help? What would the consequences be of an injury at any point along this hike, and how should you prepare for avoiding and dealing with that?

After you mulled over those questions and any others that may be relevant to the hike you're contemplating, you may decide, "Yes, I can do this!" Great! Don't be intimidated by all of this talk about safety and comfort level. The point is not to discourage you but merely to prepare you for any challenge you wish to take—whether modest or great, it's a challenge to you and that's all that matters. Go out and have fun. Just think and be safe, and you'll do fine.

Bagging Peaks

Once you've gained some confidence in your ability to find your way along a trail system, you may feel the desire to set your sights higher. Avid day hikers often venture beyond the popular trails and peaks—which to a seasoned hiker can begin to seem too crowded—to mountains that, for various reasons, receive far fewer visitors to their trails. They're lesser known for numerous reasons: They may not be among the tallest mountains in the region, have views as spectacular as more heavily tramped summits, or be as close to population centers as popular peaks.

As mentioned earlier, such less-traveled trails may provide challenges not encountered on popular trails, including a more obscure footpath, more fallen trees (or blow-downs) across the trail that you have to scramble over or around, a lack of signs at trail junctions, and fewer people around who might help if you're uncertain of your location or someone turns an ankle. These hikes require a higher level of preparation than some popular hikes or trails in local city and state parks. The chapters to follow will help you attain that level of preparation.

Yet these more out-of-the-way trails and summits also offer unique rewards—not least among them a greater challenge and sense of accomplishment, and the expansive quiet and solitude of having a summit all to yourself and your companions. Instead of seeing the same popular trails over and over, you can explore new places, adding them to your growing list of peaks reached, all while furthering your hiking skills.

As the list of summits you've stood upon continues to expand, you may find yourself accumulating quite a hiker's resume—and becoming intrigued by the idea of continuing to knock off more mountains and build upon that list while seeing new places. Soon, you find you've become a peak bagger.

Peak bagging is something like a birdwatcher's "life list" of birds seen. It's simply the practice of ticking off all the peaks on some list that hikers in the past devised because they thought a particular grouping of statistically related summits posed a worthy challenge for avid hikers. It's a goal-oriented approach to hiking—some might say a bit obsessive—and some hikers deride peak bagging for that reason. Critics also accuse peak baggers of accelerating trail erosion by pursuing their list of peaks. Actually, peak baggers can logically argue that they help disperse human impact on the mountains by climbing obscure summits rather than constantly repeating the popular hikes. Plus, peak bagging is a fun goal and fairly popular in some parts of the country, particularly in the Northeast, with hikers often taking years to finish their list—and then moving on to another list.

One of the earliest peak baggers was Bob Marshall, who later became a giant in the conservation movement in this country and helped found The Wilderness Society. Today, one of the largest federal wilderness areas in the United States is named after him: Montana's Bob Marshall Wilderness, south of Glacier National

People of all ages can enjoy hiking. Here, the author's mother bags the summit of New Hampshire's Mount Washington.

Park. In the early years of the twentieth century when Marshall was a young man, he, his brother George, and mountain guide Herb Clark decided to ascend the forty-six summits in New York's Adirondack Mountains, which were then believed to rise more than 4000 feet above sea level. They achieved their goal and helped launch a movement.

Clubs have grown up around peak-bagging objectives, and thousands of hikers have ticked off one list or another, while many more continue to work at their own list—or multiple lists. Members of the Adirondack Forty-Sixers have climbed to the summit of the forty-six Adirondack peaks first linked together by the Marshall brothers and Herb Clark. We now know four of those summits are just shy of 4000 feet, but they remain on the list out of respect for tradition. Some of those peaks are officially "trailless," though hikers have, over the years, beaten out fairly good "herd paths" to the summits. A bit to the south, the Catskill 3500 Club members boast of having bagged the thirty-five summits of New York's Catskill Mountains that top 3500 feet—as well as four of those peaks a second time in winter. Half of these Catskills summits also lack official trails, and hiking to them may require bushwhacking and navigating with map and compass.

The Four Thousand Footer Club, a branch of the Boston-based Appalachian Mountain Club, maintains records of all the hikers who officially claim to have summited all forty-eight peaks more than 4000 feet high in New Hampshire's White Mountains. The New England Hundred Highest list includes the forty-eight 4000-footers in the Whites, the five peaks in Vermont's Green Mountains and fourteen in Maine that also top 4000 feet, and the thirty-three next-highest summits throughout the region that round the list off at 100—the least of which still tops 3700 feet high.

Truly ambitious peak baggers seek out the prized Northeast 111—all of the summits in New England and in New York's Adirondacks and Catskills that are more than 4000 feet. The list originally included 111 peaks, so the name has stuck, though in recent years four more peaks have been discovered that top 4000 feet, swelling the list to 115 summits.

In the Southeast, hikers pursue completing the South Beyond 6000 list of forty peaks in the Southern Appalachians higher than 6000 feet and gaining membership in the 900 Miler Club for hiking all of the approximately 900 miles of trails in Great Smoky Mountains National Park.

The Hundred Peaks Section of the Angeles Chapter of the Sierra Club maintains a list of more than 270 suggested southern California peaks to stimulate interest in climbing them. Special recognition is given to members who climb more than 100 of the peaks on the list. For more information, contact the Sierra Club or *http://angeleschapter.org/hps.*

In Colorado, hikers go after the fourteeners, the fifty-four mountains that top 14,000 feet. The Highpointers Club seeks the unusual grail of standing atop the highest point in each of the fifty U.S. states—some of them reached on a short walk from the roadside, and others, particularly Alaska's Mount McKinley, requiring advanced mountaineering skills.

All of the peak-bagging objectives mentioned are relatively more committing and serious. You'll want to build up to goals that ambitious by first knocking off smaller mountains and easier trails. You might, for instance, begin your hiking career with a goal of hiking all the trails in the state park nearest to your home. When you believe you're ready to start pursuing summits on a peak-bagging list, pick out a list and a first hike on it that seems a reasonable goal for your level of experience and ability. Remember, these lists are prized goals precisely because they're not at all easy to achieve. Stick with it, ticking off one summit after another, and your patience will one day be rewarded when you tag that final summit on your list.

So, if you're driven by goals, there are more than a few for hikers, and if your objective isn't peak bagging, that's fine, too. Hiking should remain, first and foremost, fun. The following chapters will help you learn how to keep it fun through keeping it safe and comfortable.

Chapter 2

Gear

I know what you're thinking: "This isn't supposed to cost a lot. Why would this book devote an entire chapter to gear?" Well, don't sweat it. No, hiking doesn't have to cost a lot, and you don't have to amass a warehouse full of elaborate gear simply to head out on a trail. Despite the growth in recent years of a robust manufacturing industry and retail sector built around outdoor recreation and a profusion of boots and packs and other hardware purportedly required for exploring the outdoors, you can still lace on a pair of inexpensive hiking boots or trail shoes and enjoy the woods and mountains.

Like every other chapter, this one aims to take you as far as you want to go. How far that is may be different in your mind today than it will be tomorrow or the day after, and that's fine. If you're content with outfitting yourself as simply and cheaply as possible and never want to lay out real money to hike, this chapter will show you the path to that goal. If you decide now, or later, that there's some value to having nicer gear, then just read on.

Figuring out the gear thing really just comes down to personal choices. This chapter will help you make those choices and revise them down the road as you see fit. Here's the gist of the gear conundrum (and clothing, to be covered in Chapter 3) in a nutshell: Yes, the more expensive stuff is often better with regard to ease of use, reliability, durability, and your comfort; and no, you don't absolutely have to have it. Like many hikers, I began with the cheapest boots and pack and other gear that I could find. In time, as I hiked more and more—and, not coincidentally, made a little more money—I decided the nicer gear was worth getting because I'd use it a lot and it would have a positive effect on my hiking experience.

But I've never lost sight of the fact that hiking isn't about outfitting yourself in this year's best gear. It's still about getting out in the woods and mountains, the canyons and seashore, and the badlands and plains. It's about seeing beautiful places, listening to the expansive silence, and feeling the greatness of the land make your heart pump a little faster. Get the gear that works for you. More importantly, get out there and hike.

Hiking Boots

There are certain items in life that one always wants to ensure fit properly, otherwise the consequences are direr than in most cases of poor fit. For instance, you can probably live with a shirt that's a little big or small. However, the fit of an infant's diaper becomes more critical, and the fallout—if you'll pardon the expression—of a poor fit grows more serious.

Think of your hiking boots as being just as important as that baby's diaper when it comes to proper fit. I know it won't be a hard sell to convince you of this fact because the chances are good that at some time in your life you've worn ill-fitting shoes. Whether they were dress shoes, running shoes, casual sneakers, or even hiking boots, you've experienced firsthand (firstfoot?) the discomfort of footwear that should have never been placed on your poor, innocent pigs. We all know how unpleasant, even painful, that is. Now, imagine you're wearing those ill-fitting shoes, but you're on a mountain; your car is 4 miles away down a rocky, ankle-swallowing trail; and you have to walk all the way out. I've personally had to go miles—days, actually—down a trail in boots that didn't fit me well. It was more than 2 weeks before the blisters and bruises those boots tattooed upon my feet healed completely.

Of all the gear you will ever need or want as a hiker, nothing deserves a higher priority than your boots. You can hike without a fancy waterproof-breathable rain jacket or a $200 pack or a Global Positioning System receiver, but open up a nasty blister because your boots don't fit well and your hike comes to a screeching halt—or it grinds on interminably and painfully as you count every step back to the trailhead in those bad boots. If I'm belaboring this point, it's in hopes of driving it home: Make sure your hiking footwear fits your feet.

With that said, you don't necessarily have to buy the most expensive boots in the store to get a good fit. Can you introduce yourself to hiking by wearing running shoes or street sneakers? Yes, of course you can. There aren't any rules about what you should wear or carry when hiking. Many avid hikers have logged serious miles in rough mountains shod only in old sneakers. Understand though that those old sneakers will neither give you the traction and support of true hiking boots nor will they likely keep your feet dry in wet conditions. So there's your choice. If you decide you want boots or shoes designed for hiking, the footwear you select depends on where, when, and how much you intend to hike; what you're carrying; and most of all, your feet.

What Kind of Boots?

Go to an outdoor gear retailer and you'll probably see a mighty—and perhaps mighty dizzying—array of hiking boots on display. There are lightweight shoes that look like little more than bulked-up sneakers, mid-cut and high-cut boots, fabric and leather boots, and beefier leather boots that look like something an invasion force would wear. Which ones are right for you? First, ask yourself what you want them for and how much support you think your feet need.

A good guideline when buying hiking boots is to choose the most lightweight pair that will provide the support you need. To put it more simply, don't buy more boot than you need—besides wasting money, it's not necessarily the best thing for your feet and body. There's an axiom in the industry that every pound of weight carried on your foot (the weight of your boots) is like five pounds on your back; I've seen one knowledgeable researcher recently readjust that estimate to a ratio of six to one. Whatever the math, the point is that your legs lift and place the weight of your boots with every step. The heavier your boots, the more quickly your leg muscles grow fatigued and you slow down, and the more stress is placed on the

Mid-cut or high-cut leather boots offer more ankle and foot support than lighter shoes and are usually waterproof.

ligaments and tendons in your leg and foot joints. If you doubt that a difference of a pound or more in the weight of a pair of shoes can really matter, take two 5-mile walks around town on the same route, the first time in sneakers, the second time in boots. Even on a sidewalk, you'll feel the difference. On the rougher terrain of a trail, that difference becomes more pronounced.

How much support do you need? Many new hikers start out with a mid-cut, **midweight boot** that comes up just over the ankle. It will provide adequate ankle support, and a good pair will have enough stiffness in the heel cup and padding underfoot to give your feet all the support and protection they need if you're not carrying more than fifteen or twenty pounds (most day hikers carry less than that in mild weather). The boots I'm describing generally weigh two to three pounds per pair and come in waterproof-breathable and nonwaterproof models. If your ankles have a tendency to roll or you've suffered injuries to your feet, ankles, knees, or even your hips or back in the past, you'll almost certainly want that much support. Impact absorbed by your feet instead of your boots gets transmitted through your legs and can aggravate problems in your knees, hips, and back. If injuries are a real concern, seek professional advice about footwear.

The industry trend has been toward making hiking boots lighter and more compact, thanks to improvements in materials and construction and the realization that, especially for day hikers carrying relatively light packs, we don't need the heavy, bulky leather "waffle-stomper" boots that were the accepted footwear for much of the latter part of the twentieth century. Many avid day hikers don't even need the support of mid-cut, midweight boots. Today you'll find day hikers (climbers, etc.) wearing low-cut shoes that look like street sneakers that have been through a weightlifting program. This category of footwear sometimes has been called **approach shoes,** a term predicated upon the assumption that a special shoe was required for the delicate scrambling that rock climbers sometimes do over steep slabs and boulders to reach the base of cliffs—even though many buyers of this type of shoe probably never approach a cliff. Also known more generically as **lightweight hiking shoes** or **trail shoes,** a good pair can offer a surprising amount of support and cushion while often weighing just a couple of pounds or less, greatly reducing the exertion and stress upon your leg muscles and joints caused by heavier boots.

I often hit the trail in lightweight, low-cut shoes, and find that by relying more on the muscles and connective tissue in my legs for support than on my footwear, I effectively train my legs for hiking and, I believe, reduce the chance of injury. With that said, understand that, no matter how much these shoes improve, you'll always compromise some support and cushion by choosing them over a mid-cut, midweight boot—as well as sacrificing protection from rocks and other objects on the trail that a higher-cut boot offers your ankles. The lighter your shoes, the more you have to pay attention to where you place your feet when you hike, because you have less ankle support and cushion below your feet.

Low-cut, lightweight hiking shoes keep feet cool and are easy to walk in.

Beyond how much support your feet and legs require in footwear, think about the sort of hiking you'll do. Boots that are more supportive are advantageous on rough trails where footing is uncertain, whether you're walking over and around big rocks or traveling up and down loose dirt and stones that slide away beneath your feet. **Supportive boots** allow you the freedom to walk briskly down a good trail without worrying about where you place your feet—or at least, worrying less than you would in less-substantial shoes. Their higher cut does a better job of keeping dirt and small stones out of your boots. Their better cushion underfoot means your soles won't be as sore at the end of the day as they might be in a lighter shoe.

The advantages of low-cut, lightweight hikers, by comparison, are that they feel more comfortable and cooler. Your feet will probably perspire less. Lightweight hikers will tire your legs less quickly and probably enable you to walk faster and farther than heavier boots. They usually have better traction and give you better sensitivity to whatever is underfoot, which is particularly beneficial when scrambling through a tricky area of rocks or trying to get good purchase on a steep slab of smooth rock.

There are more choices than the general descriptions I've offered. However, unless you intend to carry twenty-five to thirty pounds or more on multiday trips into the backcountry, you don't need high-cut, stiffer backpacking boots. The outdoor industry has blurred the distinctions between categories of footwear in recent years. Today, you'll find sandals that look like running shoes, hiking shoes that look like rock-climbing shoes, and every crossover imaginable and then some. Still, if your primary interest is hiking, find shoes or boots designed for that, and stay with that principle of getting the most lightweight model you can that still provides the support you need. If you want footwear that crosses over well from hiking into scrambling off-trail or trail running, you can find that, too.

With outdoor gear (and clothing), there are always trade-offs, and nothing does everything well. The more minimalist and lightweight the shoe or boot, for the most part, the less expensive it is, too. Pricier shoes and boots also tend to be made better and are more comfortable and durable, so consider that trade-off when you look at price. Mainly, think about what performance aspects rank highest in priority for you, and then you'll find shoes or boots that are appropriate for your needs.

Different Types of Boots and Recommended Uses

Shoe or Boot Type	Weight/Pair Men's Size 9	Description	Recommended Use
Lightweight, low-cut approach shoes	1.5 to 2.5 lbs.	Sneakerlike, firm heel, thick sole with superior traction, good lateral support	Day hiking any trails or off-trail scrambling, for seasoned hikers with strong ankles
Lightweight, mid-cut boots, fabric upper (not leather or waterproof)	2 to 3.5 lbs.	Boot style; more support than lightweight shoes; thicker, firmer sole	Day-hiking trails, for beginner hikers or anyone wanting more support
Lightweight, low- or mid-cut shoes or boots, waterproof-breathable	2 to 3.5 lbs.	Same as categories above, but with a waterproof-breathable liner	Same as above; for hikers in wet climates or who hike in rain
Midweight, mid- or high-cut fabric or leather boots	2.5 to 4 lbs.	More heavy-duty boot, greater support than lightweight types, often water-proof-breathable	Day hiking or back-packing with a fairly heavy pack (25–30 lbs. or more)

Waterproof or Not?

Hikers in this country have developed a fascination with all things **waterproof-breathable (W-B)** since the term was born a couple of decades ago in reference to Gore-Tex, which was the first W-B membrane in products like jackets and boots and became a household word. Today you'll find Gore-Tex and other brands of W-B materials in many models of boots and jackets. The advent of this technology has certainly changed the world of outdoor recreation and made being outside a lot more comfortable for many people. So should everything you buy be W-B (even if you could afford it)? Certainly not. W-B clothing is addressed in Chapter 3. For now, let's stick to deciding whether to get W-B hiking boots.

First of all, here's a quick lesson in what W-B means. "Waterproof" and "breathable" are objectives that are inherently at odds with one another. To make something **waterproof,** you prevent the movement of any moisture through it. The classic example is the traditional yellow rain slicker, that stiff, plastic-feeling jacket that a hurricane's rains couldn't penetrate. Of course, if you've ever walked 10 minutes down the street wearing a rain slicker, you know it doesn't "breathe" any better than a dead squirrel beside the road.

Breathability in clothing or footwear is the ability to pass moisture—in particular, the moisture vapor released by your hard-working body. The ultimate breathable "membrane," if you will, might be the fishnet stocking. Sure, it has great movement of air and moisture through it but zero resistance to rain or any other form of precipitation, not to mention wind.

> ## Determining a Boot's Support
>
> Here's how to compare the support of different hiking shoes and boots: First, hold one boot in your hands and bend the boot's toes backward, or upward, to see how readily the boot bends in that normal direction. Second, squeeze around the heel to feel the stiffness and size of the heel cup, which is important for protecting your heel. Last, hold the boot toe in one hand and the heel in the other and twist the boot as you would wring water from a towel.
>
> Here's the trade-off: Stiffness generally translates to greater support, while suppleness is often characteristic of lighter-weight, cooler shoes. Conduct these tests with different models and you'll find a difference in the amount of stiffness and support in each, which is helpful in deciding which boots are right for you.

The great advance of W-B technology was that it introduced some breathability to waterproof items that previously did not breathe, or release moisture, at all. Thus, you could wear a jacket or boot that was waterproof, yet it would release your body's vapors as you hiked, so you wouldn't feel trapped inside a plastic bag. That was an incredible stride. Despite continued improvements in the technology, anything that keeps rain out cannot breathe as well as a fabric or membrane that is not waterproof. So anything that's W-B—whether a jacket or boot or anything else—compromises breathability to some extent. The industry has recognized the limited breathability of its W-B boots and garments—recognized that they can simply be too hot in mild temperatures—and has shifted its efforts to producing shells that are highly water-resistant but breathe much better than W-B shells (see Chapter 3).

What does this mean for you and your boots? It comes down to a trade-off between the better breathability of boots that are not W-B and the protection from water of boots that are. The design of the boot also affects how hot or cool it is. Leather boots are warmer than fabric boots, and high-cut boots are warmer than low-cut ones. A low-cut, W-B hiking shoe could be cooler than a high-cut leather boot that lacks a W-B membrane. The following are pros and cons for W-B boots. To help you choose the best pair of boots, see which qualities best match your priorities and typical hiking experience.

You may want W-B boots if the following apply:
▲ You sometimes hike in the rain, hail, or snow.
▲ Even if you usually avoid hiking on rainy days, the trails where you hike can get muddy or the vegetation is often wet.
▲ You often cross shallow streams and creeks in your boots.
▲ You hike year-round, including on cold winter days.
▲ You hike at higher elevations from spring through fall where you may encounter snow.

You may *not* want W-B boots if the following apply:
▲ You hike mostly in dry climates where rain is infrequent.
▲ You don't intend to hike on rainy days.
▲ You'd prefer the coolest pair of shoes or boots you can find.
▲ Your feet get very hot and sweaty while hiking.
▲ You don't want to pay the significantly greater price for W-B boots.

Selecting Your Boots

Feet are sort of like fingerprints—everybody's are different. Manufacturers of shoes and boots build their footwear around something called a **last,** which is essentially like a mold of a foot to which they fit their shoes (with a different-size last for each shoe size). A last used by one manufacturer may differ in shape from that used by another—enough for the fit to feel different. The trick for you is to find a company that makes shoes around a last that closely resembles the shape of your foot. Many boot manufacturers now make women's shoes and boots designed around a last that mirrors a woman's foot, which is typically more narrow than a man's. Female hikers will usually find a better fit in a women's boot.

As stressed earlier, finding a good fit is crucial to your comfort on the trail and the most important factor in selecting the right boots. That's why getting a recommendation about a particular model of shoe or boot from someone else is so difficult—that shoe may fit you differently than it fits the other person. You'll benefit from trying on a variety of boot models before buying: Only by comparing can you get a refined sense of what feels good and what doesn't. Any good retailer of outdoor gear will allow you to wear the boots in the store for as long as you feel necessary to pass judgment on the fit. Wear the socks you'd wear on a hike, and make sure the socks fit snugly and don't bunch up. Carry a pack with as much weight in it as you'll carry while hiking, put on the boots, and walk around the store for an hour or more. Go up and down stairs, and try to find a ramp to walk up and down, to simulate going uphill and downhill on a trail.

Buying hiking boots is not like buying street shoes. In a shoe or boot meant for hiking, you want enough room in the toe box to wiggle your toes and not feel them slamming against the front of the shoe when you walk downhill. A lightweight, low-cut hiking shoe flexes more when you walk than a higher-cut, more supportive boot, so you can afford a slightly more snug fit in the toes in the lightweight shoe than in the bigger boot. Still, you don't want your toes to feel crammed, or they'll get sore and possibly blister on a long downhill hike. Have at least a thumb's width of space between big and second toes and the end of the shoe. In addition, your foot should not slide forward or backward in the boot, and your heel should feel nicely embraced by the boot: The heel shouldn't move more than a quarter inch when you walk. Make sure the boot's cuff doesn't contact your ankle or shin uncomfortably when walking with the boots laced snugly. Once you've laced up the shoes or boots, you should have range in the lacing to loosen or tighten them up further. On the trail you may want to retie laces a little tighter for a long downhill, to stabilize your foot inside the boot; or similarly, lace them slightly loosely going uphill, when your foot needs to flex more. Last, always buy shoes at the end of the day, because your feet swell during the day.

After you've bought shoes or boots, wear them at home, to work for a few days (if possible), and around town before taking your first big hike in them. Although modern day-hiking shoes or boots should not be so stiff that they require break-in time, you want to be doubly certain the fit is right before committing yourself to wearing them for hours on a trail. Wearing them around town also gives your feet a chance to get accustomed to the boots. Moreover, some stores may let you return the shoes for an exchange or a refund if you realize at home that they don't fit as well as you'd thought and if you haven't worn them outside yet.

Socks—The Unsung Hero of Footwear

After your boots, there's another important, if under-appreciated, element to foot comfort while hiking: socks. You could suffer a case of sticker shock at the prices of modern hiking socks. However, getting well-fitting boots and then coupling them with cheap socks is like buying a new luxury car and installing barrels inside it for seats. Socks make a big difference, and a pair of good ones will last you several hiking seasons. If you only day hike occasionally, you'll probably only need a couple of pairs. As someone who hikes a lot and has worn good socks and cheap ones, I'll testify that the good ones are worth the money.

Most modern hiking socks combine various synthetic fabrics that stretch and wick moisture, and some use a bit of wool (merino wool is popular, comfortable, and durable). They feature extra padding under the heel and ball of the foot, where you need it, and often have a snug, elastic fit around the arch for added support. Companies label their socks as made for a variety of outdoor activities (for example, hiking, backpacking, trail running), and make models cut low, high, and everywhere in between. For day hiking with a light pack (no more than fifteen to twenty pounds) in warm to moderately cool temperatures, look for a midweight hiking sock with good padding. For cold-weather hiking, get a heavier, warmer sock and perhaps a thin liner sock to help wick moisture from your feet and add a little more insulation. If you hike in places where loose dirt and small stones cover the trails or ticks, poison ivy, thorny brush, or anything such as that is a concern, get high-cut socks.

Foot Care

You don't need to keep a podiatrist on retainer to take proper care of your feet as a hiker. Mainly, it's a simple matter of paying attention to your feet and taking a few smart precautions. If your feet hurt, there's a reason, so take the time to investigate (see Chapter 9 for more on how to deal with specific problems). Pulling off your boots and socks only takes a minute and can save you a lot of time and discomfort later.

For starters, getting boots that fit well should avoid the most-common problems, such as blisters or blackened toenails. Always start your hike with clean, dry socks. Some people even carry a second pair of socks on an all-day hike and pull on the fresh ones partway through the day. The other easy precaution to avoid foot problems is something I do whenever I stop for a rest on a hike, even if only for five or ten minutes: Take off your boots and socks and set them in the sun to dry out a bit. This airs out your feet—which feels great—besides drying them out and greatly reduces the build-up of moisture inside your boots over the course of your hike. Moisture is a leading culprit in the formation of blisters. If you're at a stream or creek, cool your feet in it (as long as it's okay to do so—for instance, the stream is not a water source for a campsite). If your feet tend to sweat a lot, use an antifungal powder on your feet and in your socks and shoes before and after, and even during, a hike. Another trick to keeping your feet cool on a hot hike is to fold the tops of your socks down over the cuffs of your boots. This creates a "chimney effect" that forces air down into your boot when you walk.

Whenever you take off your boots and socks, inspect your feet for any sign of blisters starting, indicated by a "hot spot" of skin that's brighter and redder than the skin around it and often sensitive to the touch. The more advanced the blister formation, the more distinct and sensitive the red spot; it may even start to bulge out from your flesh and fill with pus. A hot spot often begins feeling sensitive or painful while you're hiking. If you see or feel any sign of blisters forming, even preliminary signs, do something about it immediately (see Chapter 9).

If you have recurring foot problems, get professional medical advice right away. Don't let a problem persist; it won't go away by itself. Last, don't wear shoes or boots that are severely worn or give you any foot pain. Get a new pair.

Customized Footbeds

The flimsy foam inserts that come inside most hiking boots add a bit of cushioning but do nothing to stabilize your foot or reduce motion inside the boot. Many boot companies and foot specialists recommend over-the-counter or custom-fitted footbeds (called **orthotics**). **Customized footbeds** are inserts that are more supportive than those that come in most shoes and boots. They can alleviate many sources of foot pain. Good footbeds—ones with a rigid shank to absorb all the stress of bearing weight—are beneficial for the vast majority of people and inexpensive. They can improve fit, comfort, and structural stability of any boot, plus prevent foot elongation, blisters, calluses, and other short- and long-term problems.

To get a truly customized insert, one designed specifically for your foot and its problems, you'll have to see a podiatrist. There are also brands of "customized" inserts available over-the-counter, which may be worth trying because they're much less expensive than having special ones made for yourself.

Packs

If your boots are at least arguably the single most-important item of gear you'll buy, then your pack will likely be the piece of gear to which you become most attached. I mean it. Boots wear out, but a good pack can last many years. It will probably become the piece of gear you're most familiar with, given how many hours you'll spend in direct physical contact with it or going through it. Ask an avid hiker about his or her boots, and you'll hear an honest but largely emotionless assessment of their comfort and functionality. Ask the same person about his or her pack of choice, and you'll get a response that clearly comes more from the heart. Your pack matters.

Think of your pack as a tool. You want it to do more than simply fit everything you need on a hike. You want your pack to help you organize the food, water, clothing, and other stuff you're carrying to allow you quick and easy access to any particular item at any given time. Your pack should carry comfortably on your back whether completely or only partly full. So, put some thought into purchasing a pack—you'll be happy you did, because if you're like most hikers, you're liable to own and use that pack for years to come.

There's a staggering variety of packs designed for day trips available today, in many sizes, shapes, designs, and prices. What may seem an overwhelming choice becomes much easier once you consider what exactly you want a pack to do for you. Let's look at some of the different types of packs available for day hiking and their advantages.

What Kind of Pack?

To begin with, you don't want any day pack intended primarily for any use other than hiking, such as a travel pack or book bag. These items may appear to save you money, but they're not built for the amount of use and abuse that hiking packs take; they'll fall apart quickly.

The smallest category of packs for short hikes or trail runs of up to a few hours in mild weather includes fanny packs and smaller hydration packs. **Fanny packs** are just what they sound like, small, unobtrusive packs that sit atop your buttocks, with a thin belt that clips around your waist. Some of them have a holder for a water bottle or two. **Hydration packs** are water bladders inside a protective nylon sheath, or pack, with shoulder straps and a thin belt, worn on your back, with a hose running from the bladder over the shoulder strap where you can grab it at will for a quick drink (the mouth of the hose has a valve you bite on to drink from it). They come in a range of models and sizes that have different capacities for both water (or whatever fluid you want to bring along) and cargo. Fanny packs and hydration packs may have roughly 300 to 700 cubic inches (c.i.) of space—enough room for water, a little food, and a light jacket—and they range greatly in price. Either provides easy access to water, though a hydration pack is certainly more convenient in that regard, making it preferable for something like trail running. (The down side of that convenience is that you have to occasionally clean hydration bladders to remove mildew, but that's a fairly simple task.) Fanny packs and smaller hydration packs are intended for light loads of no more than a few pounds to ten pounds, depending on the model, and won't be comfortable carrying more weight than they're designed to handle.

Fanny packs, or lumbar packs, carry enough for short hikes in mild weather.

If you plan to take all-day hikes, from spring through fall, on which you'll carry food, water, and enough clothing for the range of weather you might encounter in mountains (see Chapter 3), you'll want a day pack, larger hydration pack, or lumbar pack with a capacity of about 750 to 1500 c.i.

A **lumbar pack,** like a fanny pack, has no shoulder straps, so all the weight rides on your hips—or lumbar area of your lower back, thus the name. They are fine for carrying up to ten pounds, or even fifteen pounds with better models, but carrying any more weight than that for long gets uncomfortable for your lower back. Lumbar packs differ from fanny packs in that they usually have greater capacity and are built to carry comfortably with more weight than you'd want to put in a fanny pack—thanks to good padding in the hipbelt and side stabilizer straps to pull the load into your hips. They usually have one main compartment, and possibly one or two smaller pockets inside or outside, and one or two external mesh pockets for water bottles.

Day packs have shoulder straps and a belt, and models of this size are comfortable carrying up to fifteen or twenty pounds. Most have pockets for organizing your stuff and basic exterior features such as an ax loop and daisy chains. Some

Use a full-size day pack for longer hikes when you need a lot of clothing, food, and water. Here, a hiker enjoys the Boise Foothills, Idaho.

have internal hydration—a water bladder with the hose protruding from the pack for easy access to water—or have an external pocket or two for water bottles that are within easy reach when you're wearing the pack. Day packs and lumbar packs are reasonably priced—cheaper than some of the bigger hydration packs—and there are numerous models out there.

Larger hydration packs differ from day packs in that their primary function is as a carrier of water, and secondarily, they have pockets and cargo space for other stuff. There are numerous models with a range of water and cargo capacity at a range of prices. Some are big enough for an all-day hike and in many ways ideal for that, thanks to adequate space for all the food and clothing you'll need and having water immediately accessible without having to pause in your stride and reach for a bottle.

A growing category of day packs is **specialized packs** intended for outings that require more gear and clothing than most three-season day hikes. People who may need a pack like this include hikers going out for long days in colder weather or in winter, climbers, snowshoers and cross-country skiers heading out for a day in the mountains, or a parent carrying his or her children's things. These packs have the support to comfortably carry up to twenty or thirty pounds and enough capacity (about 2000 to 3500 c.i.) for big, all-day outings. They also often sport more features than smaller, simpler day packs, especially those designed for specific activities such as climbing and backcountry skiing or snowboarding. They vary tremendously in their features, capacity, the pack's empty weight, the amount of padding and support in the hipbelt and shoulder straps, and how you access the pack's contents. Many have internal hydration and water bottle pockets. You'll spend more on these packs than on simpler day packs or lumbar packs.

A final category of day packs that will be of interest to parents of infants and toddlers is **child-carrier packs.** These consist of a cockpit for the child to sit in, attached to a regular pack frame-harness-hipbelt you'd see on any other pack. There's been a boom in this category of pack in recent years, thanks to consumer demand, so the packs have become much more comfortable to carry and much nicer for the child's ride. Fit the pack to your torso the way you would any other pack. Fortunately, many child-carrier packs adjust to a wide range of torso lengths, so you should be able to find one pack that both mom and dad can wear. Kid carriers also come in many sizes in terms of the amount of cargo space they have for extras such as food, drinks, and baby supplies. Some are big enough for backpacking and may be heavier than you need for day hiking; others have little or no space and are designed only for walking around town. One big difference between carriers designed for different purposes is the amount of support and comfort they provide for the parent—an around-town carrier often lacks the support for toting a child around for a few hours or more on the trail. Don't shortchange yourself on comfort to save a few dollars. A day-hiking kid carrier should have enough cargo space for your needs, which may vary, depending on whether you'll usually have another adult along carrying a regular day pack. Look also for a sun shade and rain shade for your child, a harness system that prevents your child from climbing out of the pack or tumbling out if you stumble, and "gear" loops within reach of the child for attaching toys.

Don't get hung up on trying to figure out what a particular measure of cubic inches translates to in terms of space in a pack. The measures provided for any pack are not always precise, anyway. If you're not sure whether a pack is big enough, fill it up in the store with the stuff you'd carry on a hike to see for yourself.

As for how much to spend, do this: Before deciding what you're going to spend, try a variety of packs of different types and sizes. Get an idea of what's out there, what you want, and what you can get for your dollar. The more packs you look at and try on, the better a sense you'll get of what will best serve you and what you think is reasonably priced. For the most part, some packs cost more for good reasons: They're more comfortable (provided you get the right fit), have more features, and are built to last. Less-expensive packs always sacrifice somewhere, usually in comfort, fit, and features, but may still be a good bargain as long as they're made well enough to last several years. After looking around thoroughly, you might spend a little more than you'd intended or possibly a little less. Either way, you'll know what you're getting and probably be satisfied.

Getting the Right Fit

Start by measuring your torso: Stand at attention and have someone extend a soft tape measure from your seventh vertebra—the prominent bone at the base of your neck—along your spine to the top of your hip bones, which you can find by placing your hands on your hips and drawing a line between your thumbs. If you don't have a soft tape measure, use a string and then hold the measured string to a yardstick.

If comfort is important to you and you intend to carry more than about fifteen pounds, look for padding in the hipbelt and shoulder straps and a back pad.

When trying on a pack, fill it with what you'll carry on the trail. Loosen the suspension straps. Buckle the belt and chest strap. With the hipbelt resting atop your hip bones, not sliding down over them, pull the belt comfortably snug. Tighten the stabilizer straps, beginning with the lowest if there's more than one. Next, tighten the load-lifters, which should lie at an angle of forty-five degrees to your shoulders. Finally, tighten the shoulder straps and chest strap as desired.

You should have leeway in the belt and all straps to loosen or tighten further. The shoulder straps should wrap cleanly around your shoulders, without gaps or bunching, and extend about a hand's width beneath your armpits. If not, you need a different suspension size.

When properly adjusted, about two-thirds of the pack's weight should ride on your hips, with the rest on your shoulders and upper back. Walk around the store wearing a loaded pack. If it doesn't feel comfortable, find another one.

On the trail, you may want to make slight adjustments for comfort in varied terrain. For instance, loosening the hipbelt and stabilizer straps slightly gives your hips and legs extra mobility for going uphill. Tightening everything stabilizes your load to prevent it throwing you off-balance going downhill.

Loading a Pack

Why not just throw everything inside the pack, right? Well, sure, you can certainly do that—you won't hurt the pack. However, it might feel lopsided when you carry it, the weight might feel too high or too low, or something sharp and hard inside might poke you in the back. In addition, when you stop for a snack or to grab a jacket, you might find yourself digging through the entire pack wondering where the #%$* you put that thing.

Loading your pack in an organized, methodical way such that the pack's load is properly distributed not only allows you to locate things quickly but also makes you much more comfortable over the course of a hike.

I have a system for loading a pack that I generally follow no matter how big the pack or how long the trip. In short, I want things that I may need quickly (for example, map, compass, light source, batteries, first-aid kit, jacket) in an accessory pocket or otherwise immediately accessible so that I'm not fumbling around looking for them when I need them right away. Items that I'll only pull out of the pack on a rest stop or longer stop, or which I don't actually anticipate needing but have just in case, can go inside the main compartment (for example, lunch, extra water and clothing). If there's a chance of rain or wind, I'll keep a jacket on top in the main compartment. Small items I place together in a tiny stuff sack and put in a smaller pocket to avoid losing them amid everything else.

When you're on a good trail, load the pack's main compartment so that most of the weight is up high, close to your shoulders, and place lighter items at the bottom. Women, whose legs are long relative to their torso, may prefer centering the weight slightly lower. If there are any hard or sharp objects that could poke you in the back, use soft items, such as a fleece jacket, to pad them. Once the pack is loaded, tighten all compression straps to prevent any shifting of the contents, which could throw you off-balance on the trail.

If you're planning some off-trail adventure, including bushwhacking or canyoneering, make sure your pack is compact and streamlined of all strap-ons for snag-free hiking. Lower the center of gravity slightly to enjoy a neutral, upright stance that lets you easily straighten up after crawling, crouching, or stumbling. Loosen the load lifters a bit to give arms greater range of motion. Tighten the sternum strap to compensate. Cinch your hipbelt tight to carry most of the weight. The shoulder straps should be tight enough to eliminate load sway during contortions and help "tow" the packbag through tangled vegetation.

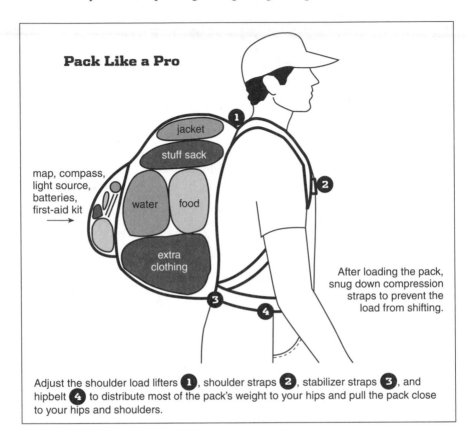

Pack Like a Pro

jacket

stuff sack

map, compass, light source, batteries, first-aid kit →

water   food

extra clothing

After loading the pack, snug down compression straps to prevent the load from shifting.

Adjust the shoulder load lifters **1**, shoulder straps **2**, stabilizer straps **3**, and hipbelt **4** to distribute most of the pack's weight to your hips and pull the pack close to your hips and shoulders.

Caring for Your Pack

A pack doesn't need a lot of TLC—a good one pretty much puts up with whatever you do to it. However, if you want your pack to last many years and still be in good shape, a little smart pack care goes a long way toward realizing that goal (and saves you spending money on a new pack sooner than you want). Clean out your pack after every trip. Unzip all pockets and compartments to shake out crumbs, dirt, sand, and other stuff such as wet clothing. If the pack is grungy, sponge it off with mild soap and water. Air dry the pack out of the sun, because ultraviolet rays damage the nylon fabric in a surprisingly short time. Inspect your pack for loose seams or deteriorating hardware at major stress points around the hipbelt, shoulder straps, and suspension stabilizers. A blown shoulder strap could mean big transport troubles deep in the woods. Repair worn zippers before they pop, otherwise you might end up with belongings strewn along miles of trail. Store your pack in a cool, dry, airy place out of direct sunlight to keep it from collecting mildew, which can delaminate the fabric's waterproof coating.

What Else Should I Bring?

Deciding what you carry on the trail depends on where you're going, how long you'll be out there, and the environment you're entering (that is, the weather and terrain you'll encounter). Two different people going to the same place may head out with different levels of preparedness: On a backpacking trip in the Colorado Rockies, as friends and I sat at a 12,000-foot mountain pass leaning against our heavy packs enjoying the view and a snack, a trail runner reached the pass wearing only shorts, a tee shirt, and a fanny pack. He was out there for a few hours and needed nothing more; we were carrying everything we needed for 5 days in the wilderness. Each of us were properly outfitted for our respective trips—we were simply on different trips in the same place.

For an hour or two on a trail in the woods of a local state park, on a mild day, you may need no more than a water bottle and light jacket in a fanny pack and maybe a map of the park if you're not familiar with its trails. For an all-day hike that takes you several miles into the mountains, whether on the Appalachian Trail or in the Sierra of California's Yosemite National Park, you'll need a higher level of preparedness. I'll elaborate later on everything you'd need for that all-day hike and how to evaluate what to bring on shorter outings depending on where you're going; some items include references to chapters that explain more about what to do with those items. Ultimately, you should make your own evaluation of what to bring based on your own experience and what you believe you (and your group) needs.

The Ten Essentials

First, the **Ten Essentials** is a widely accepted list of items considered necessary on any outing into the backcountry; some of these are for emergency use only, others you'll use on every hike:

1. Map
2. Compass
3. Flashlight or headlamp with spare bulb and batteries
4. Extra food
5. Extra clothing
6. Sunglasses
7. First-aid kit
8. Pocket knife
9. Matches in a waterproof container
10. Firestarter

Are all of these things really necessary? Consider their purposes and benefits.

A **map** and **compass** (see Chapter 6) are essential for finding your way, even on a trail you know intimately. You could still take a wrong turn or be forced to take an alternative, unfamiliar route if, for instance, someone gets hurt. A Global Positioning System (GPS) receiver can also prove critical on more remote hikes.

You may be thinking, "**Flashlight** or **headlamp**?!" No, you're not planning to be out in the woods after dark. Few people who find themselves surprised by circumstances and still on the trail as night falls planned for that. Yet it happens and can result from something as serious as a leg injury or as simple as the hike being more difficult than you'd expected. Finding your way back to your car in the dark (see Chapter 6) can be relatively easy and stress-free if you have good lights with you, or it can turn into an all-night, risky thrash through the woods without light. Bring a light for everyone, make sure the batteries in it are fresh, and carry extra batteries.

The reason for **extra food** should be obvious—and if it isn't, reread the preceding paragraph. A couple of chocolate bars or energy bars takes up little space but will taste like Thanksgiving dinner if you're starving and still on the trail. *Extra water* should be added to this list (see Chapter 4).

How much **extra clothing** (see Chapter 3) you carry should be dictated by potential weather and how far you'll get from your car or a road. Obviously, the 1-hour walk in the woods requires much less extra clothing than the all-day hike in the mountains. For outings of varying lengths between those extremes, think about possible problems that could arise, the likelihood of any of them occurring, and the consequences. Use your judgment.

Sunglasses may seem an obvious thing to bring if it's sunny and unnecessary when it's cloudy. They're on this list, though, because they are indispensable if you're going into higher mountains. At high altitudes the sun is more intense than at sea level and often is entering your eyes from multiple directions because it reflects off snow (which lingers throughout the summer in bigger western mountains and into late spring and early summer in taller eastern mountains). Too much exposure to bright sunlight—especially reflected off snow at high altitudes—can cause snow blindness, a temporary but painful condition in which the retinas of your eyes become sunburned. Sunglasses should block ultraviolet (UV) rays—which are 50 percent more intense at 10,000 feet than at sea level—provide full coverage for your eyes, and be dark enough for the light conditions you'll encounter. If you'll be on or around snow for a sustained period, you'll need glacier glasses (called **glacier goggles**), which are darker than most sunglasses and have removable black cloth shields on the sides to block glare from reaching your eyes around the corners of your glasses. Effective glacier glasses can be purchased relatively inexpensively.

The **first-aid kit** (see Chapter 9) should be considered essential anytime you'll wander a greater distance from the nearest road than you could walk or run to

Trekking poles greatly reduce stress on leg muscles and joints and help prevent against an injury.

quickly summon help. A simple **pocket knife** or multiuse tool has innumerable uses. You may only slice cheese with it on most hikes, but you'll be happy you have it if you ever have to cut fabric for bandages or rig an impromptu litter for someone who's hurt.

A fire can save lives in an emergency and greatly increase everyone's comfort level even if your situation isn't dire. Carry some **matches**—preferably wind- and waterproof—in a waterproof container such as a zipper-lock bag. A **firestarter** may be a candle or solid chemical fuel that can be used in an emergency to ignite wet wood. These items are widely available, inexpensive, small, and lightweight enough to include in a ditty bag or first-aid kit without taking up much space. You will hopefully never need it, and indeed, it may seem silly to you to even bother carrying it. However, people have gotten lost, hurt, or stranded on casual day hikes when they fully expected to be home for dinner. If you ever do need a firestarter, boy, you'll be praising your brilliance for carrying it—and so will your companions.

Other Items to Bring

Other items I sometimes carry when hiking include the following:

▲ A **hiking guidebook,** if I want to have information about the route handy or even just to read interesting human or natural history of the place; or, similarly, a **field guide** to birds, wildlife, or wildflowers and **binoculars.**

▲ **Lip balm** and **sunblock** (see Chapter 9).

▲ A **camera** (see Chapter 6).

▲ **Toilet paper** and **alcohol wipes** for cleaning my hands and doubled **zipper-lock plastic bags** for carrying out all used toilet paper and other trash (see Chapter 7).

▲ **Trekking poles,** which, when used properly, can greatly reduce the pressure and strain on leg muscles and joints, especially knees. Anyone who's had knee or other problems, or is carrying a fairly heavy pack, should really think about getting trekking poles or even just finding a stout walking stick.

▲ A form of **water treatment** (see Chapter 4) if I think there's a chance the hike could take longer than planned or if treating backcountry water for drinking makes more sense on a long hike than carrying the weight of all the water I'll need.

▲ An **umbrella.** Yes, this may seem funny, but a compact umbrella weighs very little and takes up little space in your pack yet is greatly appreciated in a downpour (see Chapter 8).

▲ An **emergency space blanket**—again, a small, virtually weightless item that is enormously useful when needed.

▲ A **cellular phone.** Some traditionalist hikers argue that there's no place in the backcountry for cellular phones, that they represent the very thing we go into the woods and mountains to escape. Others say a cellular phone provides a vital communication link in an emergency. I say both camps are correct. I have carried a cellular phone into the mountains and have used one in an emergency and been in an emergency when I didn't have one and wished I did. Most of the time I don't have a cellular phone, and I would not use one to make casual calls in the midst of other hikers. Respect the wishes of other hikers who would be offended to see or hear someone speaking on a cellular phone in a pristine place. Let's face it, if you can't go hiking for a few hours without talking on the phone, you should rethink why you're going hiking in the first place. Keep the phone turned off when not in use to preserve your batteries and avoid having it ring unexpectedly and disrupting someone's reverie. Make your own decision about whether you want to carry one in case of emergency. In most backcountry areas—away from civilization, especially in steep terrain—you won't pick up a cellular signal anyway. Never think of a cellular phone as a substitute for good judgment or any other piece of emergency gear.

Common sense will tell you that you don't need to head out for a 2-hour walk in the woods prepared for an assault on a Himalayan peak. Then again, if you're on the fence about whether you really need something on a particular hike, balance the potential need for it and its relative importance (for instance, an emergency item) against how much of a burden it is to carry. Most of the things mentioned earlier are so small and lightweight that there's no good reason to leave them behind. If you think you might need it, that's often good enough reason to bring it.

Checklist of Items to Bring Hiking

For a short hike (a few hours or less) in a local park or forest, bring along the following:

▲ Map (unless a map is posted frequently along the trails or signs indicate where to go)
▲ Compass (see note for map)
▲ Sunglasses and a sun hat (depending on season and weather)
▲ Lip balm and sunblock (depending on season and weather)
▲ Water and (optionally) a snack

For an all-day hike of several miles, bring the items above plus the following:

▲ Flashlight or headlamp with spare bulb and batteries
▲ Extra food
▲ Extra clothing
▲ First-aid kit
▲ Pocket knife
▲ Emergency space blanket
▲ Toilet paper, alcohol wipes, and doubled zipper-lock bags
▲ Hiking guidebook (optional)
▲ Camera (optional)
▲ Trekking poles (optional)
▲ Form of water treatment (optional)
▲ Cellular phone (optional)
▲ Umbrella (optional)
▲ Matches in a waterproof container and firestarter

Chapter 3

Clothing

Like gear, clothing is something that you need, and yet you can make do without rushing out and racking up debt on your credit card to outfit yourself in the newest, nicest duds. That stuff you can acquire when you see the need or feel the desire to have it, if you ever do. Honestly, I wear good, modern technical clothing when I go hiking these days; however, when I first started hiking, and for some years afterward, my wardrobe consisted of whatever I owned already or could afford—which wasn't much. I can't think of any single item of clothing that I now wear that I couldn't absolutely hike without.

You can hike without all that fancy stuff and still enjoy yourself tremendously, especially on wooded trails where you're less exposed to the weather. As noted in Chapter 2, hiking isn't about buying all the best outdoor products, and it never should be about that. You're arguably better off gaining some hiking experience before you go out and spend money on clothing or gear, because your experience will refine your sense of what you want. However, you should understand that the quality of your clothing can make a big difference in your comfort level in certain conditions—not on a warm, sunny, windless day, of course, but certainly on a cold, wet, windy day. You should understand the limits of any clothing you have and not attempt a hike that may expose you to severe weather with inadequate clothing. At best, that may be miserable, and at worst it can be dangerous.

Many summer hikes require only shorts and a tee shirt, though avoid cotton garments.

Skin to Shell, Sunny to Soggy: Layering and Temperature/ Moisture Management

There are a couple of truths about hiking in the woods and mountains that at first blush seem contradictory: (1) You can get very wet and cold, and (2) with the right clothing and a little knowledge of how to dress, you can go out in pretty darn bad weather and remain warm and relatively—or completely—dry.

If that seems improbable, well, just a few decades ago it still was. Since the advent and continual improvement of synthetic fabrics that are waterproof and breathable, that breathe and wick perspiration so efficiently that they rarely get damp and dry incredibly quickly, or that cut wind while still breathing so well that your sweat hardly builds up inside, enduring the elements on a hike has been rendered almost easy. You don't have to hole up indoors just because there's a threat of rain—or even if it's already raining—or because it's cold, snowing, or windy. In some parts of North America, light rain or mist is an almost constant condition for entire seasons, and plenty of people still routinely go out hiking and trail running. They just dress for it.

Dressing for outdoor activities such as hiking simply requires an understanding of a term you've no doubt heard: **layering.** You want to select an assortment of layers that keeps you comfortable and warm enough, or cool enough, through the range of weather you might encounter. This is achieved through adding an appropriate layer (or more) when you're too cold and also—very importantly—removing a layer or layers when you're too warm.

Garments should fit together well when worn in combination, that is, each layer is slightly more loose-fitting than the layer worn underneath it. Of course, you don't have to put on and remove garments in any particular order, and the most versatile and useful pieces can be worn in a variety of combinations with other things and still fit well, without restricting your movement. You'll actually get the most use out of relatively less-expensive base layers (worn against the skin, such as a tee shirt) and lightweight middle layers (for example, a fleece vest or jacket) that are highly breathable—you'll wear that jersey constantly and wear the fleece alone over the jersey or as a middle layer beneath another jacket. The classic natural-world analogy to layering is the humble onion: Peel back its layers of skin and you find none are individually thick—yet, layered together, they create a formidable shell.

Rain and cold aren't deterrents to hiking when you're prepared, as these hikers prove on Vermont's Mount Mansfield.

You may get wet on a hike so wear clothing that dries quickly or bring a change of clothes.

Ideally, your layering system consists of as few garments as necessary, thus representing minimal weight, bulk, and expense. How many pieces of clothing you get and how functional each is in terms of versatility in varying weather depends on your budget, and how much you need also depends in part on the climate and environment where you'll hike.

The point about removing layers when you're too warm can't be overemphasized. We instinctively add layers when we feel cold, but some hikers neglect to remove layers when they're overheating. The problem with overdressing is that you'll sweat a lot, possibly overwhelming the ability of even the most-breathable clothes to move all that perspiration off of your body and into the air. Eventually, you get very wet. Once wet, you experience conductive cooling—the moisture on your skin and clothing conducts heat away from your body, accelerating the cooling process. Although that's actually a good thing in hot weather—as anyone who's emerged wet from a quick dip in a creek on a hot day knows—below around fifty-five degrees Fahrenheit (this varies between individuals and depends on your exertion level), your body can no longer produce heat fast enough to compensate for the loss of body heat through conductive cooling. Despite all the warm clothing you're wearing, you get cold—and you've rendered that clothing ineffective at helping you warm back up because it's wet.

The lesson here: Drop as many layers as necessary to avoid sweating heavily, even if it means hiking in your jersey on a cool day—which isn't all that unusual for someone going uphill at a strong pace. Conversely, when that person starts downhill and her exertion level suddenly declines, she'll soon need to add warm layers. In cool temperatures, your goal is to find a balance between your exertion level (or your production of body heat) and the air temperature and wind level (which deprive your body of its precious heat) at which you feel warm but are perspiring minimally or not at all. Often that means either starting your hike dressed not quite warmly enough and warming up soon through exertion or stripping off a layer about 10 or 20 minutes into your hike once you've warmed up.

On a hot day, it may be impossible to avoid sweating, especially when walking uphill; but if it's that hot, getting cold may not be a concern unless your hike brings you from hot, windless forest to high above the trees, where you're exposed to cold mountain winds. In this scenario, you need a **jacket** that blocks the wind, yet breathes well enough that you won't overheat inside it (see more later about today's high-tech clothing). Having a **synthetic shirt** that dries quickly also becomes extremely helpful in this situation. With both, you'd just pull the jacket on over the jersey and keep hiking; in minutes, the jersey will be dry. Lacking the quick-drying shirt, carry a spare, dry shirt in your pack to change into once you get above tree line and you're beyond the stretch of the hike where you'll sweat heavily.

Let's go back to that hot-day scenario. Too much heat can make you ill (see Chapter 9), and we know the dangers of too much exposure to ultraviolet (UV) rays, which are more powerful and dangerous at higher elevations. Going shirtless is not beneficial to cooling yourself down on a hot day, and it obviously doesn't protect you from UV exposure. As mentioned earlier, that damp shirt helps cool your skin through conductive cooling, and it does so more effectively than your skin's surface, even when your skin is damp with perspiration. Keep your shirt on, and use sunblock on exposed skin. Wear a sun hat to keep the sun off your head, especially at higher elevations.

Then there's rain. Hike enough and someday you will get rained on. Few people look forward to it, but it's not that bad if you're prepared for it. Here's where you'll appreciate a good rain jacket that breathes and ventilates well. **Waterproof-breathable (W-B) jackets** can get steamy in a warm rain or even in temperatures in the fifties and forties if you're working fairly hard. Often, you won't need anything but a base layer under the jacket, and you'll want to open its vents (such as armpit zippers) to avoid overheating. Moderating your pace can also help prevent overheating.

Anticipate the need to adjust layers and do so before you get too hot or cold. For instance, as soon as you break out above tree line into a cool wind, you'll begin rapidly cooling off. Don't wait until you feel it—pull on the jacket while your body is still warm, and you'll warm that jacket. In winter or on cold autumn days, especially, your body cools quickly and takes more time and energy to warm up; add the layers before the cooling accelerates and you'll avoid that long cooling-and-warming process. Similarly, when you feel yourself getting warm walking uphill, don't wait until you're perspiring freely to remove a layer: Let your body reach a comfortably warm temperature, but strip off a layer or two before you start sweating. If you stop even for 5 or 10 minutes in cool air, pull on a jacket while resting.

Cool Stuff

I field-test a lot of new technical garments for *Backpacker* magazine, and I'm impressed every year by much of it. The outdoor industry continues to make being outside in difficult weather increasingly more comfortable. By **technical garments,** I'm referring to base, middle, and outer layers that are designed to transport moisture from your body into the air (or "breathe"), dry quickly, and in some cases trap heat efficiently relative to their weight and bulk and protect you from wind and precipitation. That these garments achieve all this while continually getting more lightweight, comfortable, and affordable makes them all the more appealing to recreational hikers.

Base layers are short-sleeve and long-sleeve shirts, underwear and bras, long underwear, and shorts and pants that are worn against your skin. These fabrics carry many names, some of them proprietary to specific manufacturers, and most are some type of nylon or polyester. Some fabrics wick perspiration and dry more quickly than others, but they change and improve too frequently to review them here (see *Backpacker* magazine for current information). They also differ in how warm they are and in their design and features. You may want separate base layers for warm and cool weather.

Middle, or **insulating, layers** come in many forms, and many of these garments are versatile—you'll get a lot of wear out of good ones for their cost. This category includes everything from lightweight fleece vests and jackets to windproof fleece, lightweight wind shells that shed nothing heavier than a light rain but breathe much better than W-B jackets—making them better for when your body's working hard—and, of course, traditional wool vests and jackets and garments that marry wool with a synthetic fabric. These actually function as both middle, insulating layers and as outer layers, depending on the weather. On a cool but dry hike you may wear only one of these garments over a base layer. You'll also layer them under a rain jacket in cold, wet weather.

Outer layers, or **shells,** are the W-B jackets and pants designed to allow the tiny molecules of water vapor rising from your pores to escape the garment, while keeping the larger molecules of rain and other precipitation out. The waterproof part is easy—it's marrying breathability to something waterproof that's the great trick and creates the expense. Manufacturers keep striving to improve the breathability of these garments, because they can get too hot when you're hiking in mild temperatures. W-B garments are usually treated with a durable, water-repellent finish (DWR), which is what causes water to bead up and run off them. If you feel you need a breathable rain jacket but never expect to encounter cold temperatures, look for one of the more lightweight W-B jackets with good ventilation, such as zippers under the armpits and chest pockets lined with mesh to allow air move-

Synthetic jerseys with a partial front zipper let you ventilate when you're working up a sweat and keep you warm when it's chilly.

Synthetic nylon pants with zip-off legs let you quickly adjust to changing temperatures.

When hiking in sunshine, especially at higher elevations, wear a hat to protect against the sun.

ment. Some models now weigh a pound or less and aren't as hot as jackets and parkas intended for winter use.

A good idea on any hike in hot weather is a **sun hat.** If you expect heavy rain, consider a rain hat with a wide brim that will keep the rain from infiltrating your jacket (unless your jacket has a good hood that seals snugly around your face, with a brim that keeps the rain off your face). In cool weather, always carry a **warm fleece** or **wool hat** in case it turns chilly, because your head is a major avenue for heat loss from the body and a hat retains a lot of heat relative to its bulk and weight. I always carry a **windproof fleece earband** in cool weather to keep my ears warm while allowing my head to cool while I'm moving. **Silk** or **synthetic glove liners** are almost weightless but help in a pinch should a storm blow in or you get caught outside overnight. One last item that comes in handy in rain or snow is a pair of **gaiters,** which wrap around your lower legs above your boots to keep precipitation from getting your feet wet. They are usually made of nylon and are waterproof or water-resistant and preferably breathable. Gaiters come in low-cut lengths (rising just above the ankle) for warmer weather hikes in rain or someplace where you might cross snow and high-cut lengths for cold weather and deep snow.

With many technical garments, whether base, middle, or outer layers, durability walks hand in hand with weight to some extent. The lighter and thinner the fabric, the more quickly it's likely to wear and the more susceptible it is to tearing on sharp edges. Of course, base layers get worn more than anything else, so you'll replace them most often. A good W-B jacket should last through several years of

In the mountains, the wind or temperature can be chilly even in a warm sun. Here a hiker is dressed for warmth on Knife Edge Trail on Maine's Mount Katahdin.

moderate use before its breathability is compromised and it starts appearing to soak up water—known as **wetting out**—rather than shedding it. This compromised performance is usually caused by dirt, smoke from wood fires, and oils from your skin infiltrating the jacket's fabric or by deterioration of the fabric from long-term exposure to UV rays. You can slow everything but UV degradation by washing the jacket. Check the manufacturer's recommendations on washing. Often, the heat of a normal dryer cycle helps to reactivate the DWR, but some garments should be dried on low heat. If the DWR has worn off, washing and drying won't restore it, but you can purchase products designed to restore a DWR to a jacket or pants. Again, see what the manufacturer recommends for this.

Don't forget, you've paid good money for your technical garments, and most manufacturers stand behind their products and will repair or replace anything that fails, within reason, unless you caused the failure. Contact the manufacturer's customer service department. Phone numbers (many are toll-free) are available at your local outdoor gear shop, in magazine advertisements, and on the World Wide Web.

What Should I Buy?

That can seem a puzzling question given the plethora of outdoor clothing out there. As with buying boots and packs, though, selecting the clothing that's right for you comes down to the sort of hiking you intend to do.

Let's revisit our hypothetical hikers from Chapter 1: Cher, Elvis, and Madonna.

Scenario 1: Cher has discovered she loves hiking small, accessible mountains with well-marked and well-maintained trails. However, she waits for fair weather to hike, preferring to avoid rain, and restricts her hiking season to between late spring and early fall, when temperatures on the hills she hikes are typically mild to hot. She almost invariably hikes uphill in a tee shirt and shorts or pants alone or with only a light layer over the tee shirt. On the summit's fairly limited area of rocky ledges above tree line, she may encounter some chilly wind but not for long.

Wardrobe 1: Cher is not exposing herself to severe weather and consequently doesn't need much in the way of technical clothing. In fact, she could conceivably wear an old cotton tee shirt and the shorts or pants she wears to the gym to hike up her hills and bring a cheap, light windbreaker for the summit when needed and a change of tee shirt in case she's gotten her first one wet with perspiration. She'll be much more comfortable, though, wearing a lightweight, short-sleeve synthetic tee shirt that wicks perspiration efficiently and dries quickly. For the coolest temperatures and winds she encounters, she needs nothing more than a lightweight, highly breathable wind shell, which would also repel a light shower; a jacket that stuffs into one of its own pockets and fits inside a fanny pack would be most convenient. Also, more convenient and functional than the shorts or tights she wears to the gym would be a simple pair of lightweight nylon hiking pants with zip-off legs.

Scenario 2: To his credit, Elvis dropped the extra weight he'd been carrying around his waistline and has become an avid day hiker, regularly venturing onto trails up mountains that bring him above tree line for long periods. He even does a little backpacking, spending up to 5 days wandering the mountains. He hikes year-round, though not too often in winter, therefore he has to be prepared for temperatures ranging from very warm to well below freezing, strong winds, rain, snow, hail, sleet—the works.

Wardrobe 2: For the type of hiking Elvis does, he requires more protective and versatile clothing than Cher. The old cotton tee shirt and shorts don't make sense for him, except perhaps on those occasional hikes where he knows he won't encounter cool temperatures, wind, or rain. For comfort as well as safety on most of his hikes, Elvis needs clothing that doesn't hold the moisture his body creates and that protects him from severe weather—and equally important, can take him from a hot, sweaty hike uphill in the woods to a cold, snowy, windy summit a few hours later. He wants a lightweight, short-sleeve synthetic tee shirt for warm temperatures and, when it's colder, a long-sleeve synthetic midweight or heavyweight jersey, preferably a pullover with a partial front zipper to vent when he's warm. For cool temperatures and wind, he'll want a versatile combination of pieces that provide warmth and wind protection and insulation under a shell, such as a fleece vest and a windproof fleece jacket with armpit zippers or other good ventilation, or a lightweight, highly breathable wind shell with a fleece or synthetic-fill vest. For the wettest, coldest conditions, and often simply for wind protection and warmth on winter hikes, he'll want a W-B

Checklist of Hiking Clothing

In warm, dry weather, bring the following:
- ▲ Tee shirt (preferably synthetic)
- ▲ Shorts or pants with zip-off legs (preferably synthetic)
- ▲ Synthetic or wool socks
- ▲ Lightweight boots
- ▲ Lightweight wind shell
- ▲ Sun hat

In cool, wet weather, bring the items above plus the following:
- ▲ Long-sleeve shirt (preferably synthetic)
- ▲ Synthetic or fleece pants
- ▲ Warm insulating layers, such as a fleece jacket or vest
- ▲ W-B rain jacket and pants
- ▲ W-B boots
- ▲ Warm fleece or wool hat or earband
- ▲ Lightweight or liner gloves or waterproof gloves or overmitts
- ▲ Wide-brimmed rain hat (optional)
- ▲ Low- or high-cut gaiters (optional)

jacket with a hem that keeps rain off his butt, a fully adjustable hood that shields his face well, and good ventilation.

Scenario 3: Madonna, our adrenaline junkie, finds inner peace on fast, long day hikes into the mountains. Hiking from late spring through autumn, she frequently gets up above the trees, into frosty winds and sometimes rain, hail, or light snow. She concludes her hiking season before winter really settles into the high elevations and avoids hiking when the forecast calls for severe cold and heavy precipitation, so she isn't likely to see heavy snowfall or wind chills well below freezing (see Chapter 8).

Wardrobe 3: With her inclination to approach hiking as an aerobic workout, Madonna needs lightweight layers that wick and dry efficiently: A lightweight short- or long-sleeve base layer and a lightweight, highly breathable wind shell may be the two things she wears most. Beyond those, a lightweight fleece vest or pullover that can be worn alone over the shirts or layered underneath the wind shell will add warmth when needed. Alternatively, to save a few dollars, she might get a windproof fleece jacket with plenty of venting instead of the fleece vest and wind shell, though one garment won't be useful in as wide a range of conditions as two. Finally, a lightweight W-B rain jacket—lighter than what Elvis needs, with perhaps a slightly shorter hem and fewer features so it's not as hot—should get her through the worst wet stuff she sees.

Cher, Elvis, and Madonna may be seeking clothing for different situations, but they'll all benefit from these tips when shopping around:

- ▲ Find clothing that fits the way it's supposed to—a garment that's too big or small for you, even if the fit seems "pretty close," will not perform as well as it should, and you're paying too much for this stuff to settle for a mediocre fit.
- ▲ The more lightweight each garment is, the cooler and more versatile it is in a variety of layering combinations, and in adapting to a range of temperatures and weather conditions.
- ▲ If you want warmth from a garment, get a dark color; if you want it to be cool in warm weather, get a light color.
- ▲ Don't pay for something you don't need. Design features in clothing add to its price; if you don't expect to need them, look for an article of clothing that better meets your needs. Shop around.

How Much Should I Spend?

Certainly not more than you can afford. If I've tried to hammer home one point in this chapter and the last chapter, it's that you don't need nice new stuff to go hiking. Beyond the realities of your budget, again, think simply about what exactly you need, using the tips and guidelines spelled out earlier. The first rule of shopping economically for outdoor clothing (or gear) is to avoid buying more than you need in any product. For instance, some makers of outdoor clothing produce impressive

W-B jackets loaded with features such as waterproof zippers, armpit zippers, and mesh-lined chest pockets for ventilation; stretch fabric in places such as the shoulders, sides, and upper arms; and fully adjustable hoods. These garments breathe well and keep you absolutely protected from any weather while allowing you to move without feeling at all encumbered. They also often cost upwards of $300 to $400, and the fact is, those jackets are designed for serious climbers; most day hikers don't need that kind of jacket. A much more basic but functional W-B rain jacket will not only do the trick but may actually be more comfortable for a day hiker in one respect: A lightweight rain jacket won't be as hot as one of those all-mountain shells. So spending big bucks can actually be counterproductive.

Do you need a W-B jacket? You may want one if you expect to hike in the rain. But you don't need one if you never hike in bad weather—or if rain is possible, you choose hikes that enable you to get back to your car quickly. A cheap rain slicker that doesn't breathe keeps the rain off you, but you'll perspire heavily if you walk far in it. W-B jackets were designed for people who will be moving in rain, cool or cold temperatures, and wind for a sustained period—the sort of weather you can encounter in virtually any mountains. If that's the kind of hiking you plan to do, think seriously about getting a decent W-B jacket.

The second and only other rule about buying outdoor clothing is this: Don't stress out about it, and don't buy something you're not sure you need. Unless you're anticipating a severely wet or cold welcome from Ms. Nature, going for a modest hike without fancy duds won't imperil your life. At worst, you might find the experience of hiking with inadequate clothing uncomfortable, in which case you'll know better afterward what clothing you need in the future.

Chapter 4

Water and Food

There's no denying the importance of these two items: water and food. Then again, devoting an entire chapter to discussing them might seem as much like overkill as would devoting an entire chapter to relieving oneself in the woods (that's Chapter 7). There are good reasons for addressing nutrition and hydration on the trail (both of which sound suddenly much more important when you use words such as "nutrition and hydration" instead of "food and water"). Must you read this entire chapter before going for a hike? Of course not. However, if you come back from that hike surprised by your unquenchable thirst or voracious appetite, or during the hike you experience an abrupt decline in your energy level or a little light-headedness from the heat, you might sit down to this chapter with a new appreciation for the subject matter and read some logical reasons to think a little harder about what you eat and drink on the trail than you would, say, at work.

Walking may not seem particularly strenuous—you may never even find your-self short of breath while on a hike. However, hiking more than a few miles, especially up and down a mountain, consumes significant amounts of energy stored in your body, and that amount really adds up over the course of several hours. You also perspire, exhale, and urinate your body's storage capacity for fluids during a hike of a couple of hours or more. Your body requires replenishment of those

Taking a break on the trail provides a chance to rest your feet while fueling up with a snack and drink.

fluids—and the hotter the temperature, the harder you're working, and the farther you hike, the more fluids you need to consume during the hike.

Becoming a Heavy Drinker

The average adult needs to drink about two liters of water per day when not performing strenuous activities—that's just to sit at your desk or read a book. Any kind of exertion increases your body's fluid needs by 50, 100, or even 200 percent or more. Factors that affect how much more fluid you'll need include how hard you're working and for how long, temperatures at either extreme of hot or cold, very high or very low humidity, and long-term exposure to the sun. The bigger you are, the more water you need.

Your rate of perspiration isn't necessarily a good indicator of how much you need to drink, either. Your body loses fluid in cold temperatures faster than you think based on how relatively little you may perspire. Nor is thirst a good indicator. Think of your thirst sensation as sort of like an "idiot" oil warning light on a car's dashboard—that light doesn't go on until your engine's oil volume has dropped much lower than it should. Similarly, if your mouth feels dry, you're already dehydrated and have not been consuming enough fluids for some time. The best way to know you're drinking enough is that you have to urinate regularly, and your urine is clear rather than yellow or even darker in color (see Chapter 9). If you go an unusually long period without feeling the need to pee, you are definitely not drinking enough.

Why worry about how much you're drinking? Water is essential to your body's life-support systems. Water helps maintain proper pressure in your cells, enabling them to metabolize the nutrients that maintain your energy level. Water keeps your kidneys functioning the way they should. Because water is a component of blood, as the water in your system decreases, so does your blood volume. Imagine your blood thickening, like oil. Less blood volume means less oxygen reaching your muscles, which can cause cramps and soreness either during your hike or workout or hours afterward. Sweating can cause an imbalance in your electrolytes, and muscles won't properly contract and relax without a balanced ratio of electrolyte minerals (for example, sodium, potassium, magnesium, calcium). Your body loses sodium through sweat, and without replacing it, you can bring on an electrolyte imbalance.

As anyone who runs, hikes, bicycles, cross-country skis, or participates in any number of high-exertion activities knows, it's hard to stay hydrated when you're working hard. That's because you can lose fluids rapidly through your urine, sweat, and breath, yet your body can only absorb water at a rate of roughly 1 to 1.5 liters per hour. In other words, guzzling a bottle of water all at once will only result in you peeing out much of that fluid a little later, without having absorbed much of it.

To keep yourself hydrated, you have to drink water or electrolyte-replacement sports drinks frequently. That's only going to happen if you keep water within easy reach, such as in a hydration pack. If you're working hard, especially if you're perspiring heavily, take several gulps of water every 15 minutes.

I know what some of you are probably thinking: You'd rather not have to pee while hiking. When you have to drop your drawers and squat to pee outdoors, it can actually seem like a good idea to not drink enough and thus not have to pee. Don't fall into the trap of this kind of thinking. Drinking so little that you actually stop urinating is dangerous (see Chapter 9). Peeing outside is also not as terrible as some people think. Really. I'll elaborate on that glamorous subject in Chapter 7.

Carrying Enough Water

If water weighed next to nothing or could somehow be concentrated or dehy-drated—"just add water to get water"—this section could be reduced to a single sentence: "Carry far more water than you expect to drink." But, alas, water is a heavy substance: One liter weighs a bit more than two pounds. Although that might not seem like much, it adds up when you're taking a long hike and you're already carrying weight in clothing, food, and gear.

Still, most day hikers find it convenient and easy to carry all the water they anticipate needing on a day hike. They avoid the need to treat any source of drinking water in the backcountry and have the reassurance of knowing the water came from a clean, reliably safe source. The amount needed on a day hike is usually one to three liters, depending on the hike's length, how hot it is, how hard you'll exert yourself, and perhaps other factors such as elevation. Even three liters doesn't add an onerous weight burden to a day pack for a hike of several hours. If your hiking route will take you past backcountry huts or any reliable source of treated drinking water where you could replenish your supply, that might allow you to start your hike with only the water you'll need to reach that source—assuming you're certain you'll get there.

Here are some tips on deciding how much water you'll need on a hike:

▲ On a mild day (temperature below about seventy degrees Fahrenheit), plan to drink about a liter every 2 to 3 hours if you're hiking at a moderate, comfort-able pace.

▲ On a hot day (temperature above about seventy degrees Fahrenheit), especially if you'll spend a lot of time exposed to direct sunlight, increase your consump-tion to approximately a liter every 90 minutes to 2 hours.

▲ Always carry a little more than you anticipate needing, just in case an emer-gency or something unexpected develops that slows you down.

▲ If you're thirsty, drink. If you discover you haven't brought enough water with you, revise your hiking plan as needed to either get more water or finish your hike before the water shortage becomes a problem. If you really need to drink, better to take your chances drinking from a backcountry source such as a stream rather than letting yourself become severely dehydrated. Still, consider what you're drinking from. If you drink from a mountain stream, you're prob-ably not too far from its source and are at less risk of getting ill than, say, drinking from a major river that's traveled many miles (and possibly picked up dangerous chemicals or metals from agricultural or mining runoff) to reach the point where you're standing.

Bottles and Hydration Systems

There are two common ways to carry and drink water while hiking: the traditional **plastic water bottle** and **hydration systems.** The latter is essentially a bladder inside a small pack with a hose extending over your shoulder and a bite valve at the end of

Drink often, drink a lot: Staying hydrated on the trail is important to staying healthy and happy.

the hose. As discussed in Chapter 2, hydration packs come in many sizes and designs, and their great advantage is allowing you to drink at will without stopping for a moment to reach for a bottle and drink from it. They are simple to use. Having such easy access to water helps ensure you consume enough fluids and drink frequently. The largest hydration packs hold enough water for several hours of rigorous activity—certainly enough water for any day hike. Their disadvantages are that (1) you usually can't readily tell how much water you have left without opening the pack and looking at the bladder, (2) the hose or bite valve could freeze

in temperatures below freezing, and (3) some bite valves are prone to leaking. However, for many people, whether heading out for an hour-long hike or trail run or an all-day tromp up and down a mountain, the advantages of hydration packs far outweigh their disadvantages.

Water bottles come in a variety of types, from bicycling bottles with valves on the caps that close up tightly to the ubiquitous hard plastic bottles with screw-top caps (for example, Nalgene bottles). These bottles are marked off in metric and English measures, which can be convenient for mixing an energy drink or measuring water for cooking in the backcountry. Water bottles with a wide mouth do not freeze as readily as a hydration pack's bite valve or any small cap or drinking valve. These bottles also allow you to see how much water you have. Plastic drink bottles bought in stores can be reused; some come with valves on the caps that can be closed, which saves you the few bucks for a one-liter hard plastic bottle. However, these drink bottles aren't as durable hard plastic ones, especially after being subjected to a lot of exposure to ultraviolet (UV) rays or subfreezing temperatures. If you prefer water bottles, make sure your pack allows you to reach your bottle without having to take the pack off; that way, you're more likely to drink frequently. Still, drinking from a bottle while hiking isn't quite as convenient as a hydration system.

Don't Drink the Water?

You might logically wonder why anyone would carry much water on a hike when, in many places, there's an abundance of water in streams and creeks. Well, the dirty truth is that the stream that appears to be so clear, sparkling, and pristine may be harboring microscopic critters that could make you wish you'd never been born with your gastrointestinal parts. For hikers, public enemies Nos. 1 and 2 are **crypto,** or *Cryptosporidium,* a microscopic, waterborne parasite that the federal Center for Disease Control and Prevention has tagged a major health risk, and *Giardia lamblia,* another waterborne parasite that, if ingested, can cause **giardiasis,** also known as **backpacker's diarrhea.**

Crypto is easily transmitted in drinking water but can be passed along just as easily by an infected hiking partner's dirty hands. Still, it occurs infrequently. Typically only long-distance trekkers become afflicted with giardiasis in the field; it takes 1 to 3 weeks (an average of 9 days) after swallowing the little bugs before symptoms show up that include loose and foul-smelling stool; cramps; rotten-egg burps; and a loss of energy, appetite, and weight. Giardiasis is often treated with antibiotics, but there is no medication proven to help overcome cryptosporidiosis. The body eventually just has to rid itself of the parasite.

Don't panic thinking you're going to have diarrhea for weeks after going hiking. I've hiked and backpacked for years without getting ill from a backcountry water source. If you drink only water that you've brought from a reliable source in civilization—such as your home tap—and make sure your hands and those of your

companions are clean when handling food, you can skip over this section. However, if you want to drink from a backcountry source, read on, knowing that backcountry diarrhea is almost entirely preventable.

Disinfecting Your Drinking Water

Begin by disinfecting all wilderness drinking water through boiling, filtration, or halogenation. **Boiling** is the safest way, and water need only reach the boiling point to be rendered free of diarrhea-causing critters. Boiling requires you to carry a stove, fuel, and pot, for which most day hikers really have no need. If you plan to cook in the backcountry, though, treating water by boiling it is the most efficient method, and there's no need to filter or otherwise treat water you intend to boil. Filtration is most convenient for day hikers, and the method is most effective when the filtering device has been proven to remove protozoa, bacteria, and viruses. Portable water filters and purifiers are widely available in outdoor gear retail stores and other retailers. Halogens (iodine and chlorine) are the least effective means of treating water because of the variable results based on things such as the concentration of the halogen, contact time with the germs, clarity of the water, temperature of the water, and questionable efficacy of iodine and chlorine against *Cryptosporidium*.

Filters physically strain out offending critters larger than a size given for the particular filter product. Some filters remove, or filter out, protozoa and bacteria,

Pump filters let you treat water in the backcountry. These filters require only pumping a handle for a few minutes to fill a bottle with treated water.

and there are filters that "purify," which means they remove viruses, too. Which type you choose depends on the degree of risk you're willing to take. Obviously, **purifiers** are the safer way to go because they strain out the hard-to-get viruses, but they cost more and tend to clog more quickly than nonpurifiers. All filtering devices clog eventually, some sooner than others. Because a plugged-up filter does you about as much good as a tent without a roof, this is an important factor to consider when shopping.

Treating water through **halogenation** entails using either iodine, which comes in tablet, crystal, and liquid forms, or liquid drops of chlorine dioxide. Iodine is lightweight, cheap, and as easy as dropping a sugar cube into a cup of coffee. But if you're dealing with murky, foul-tasting water, iodine does nothing to make it more appealing, and iodine itself adds a taste to water that many people find foul, although it is now often sold with companion tablets that remove the iodine taste. More importantly, experts recently discovered that iodine doesn't kill *Cryptosporidium.* Two manufacturers make the chlorine dioxide drops, McNett and Aqua-Lung, and both claim that when mixed correctly, they take care of *Giardia* and crypto.

Fueling Your Engine

Many people find it unnecessary to eat on a hike of less than 2 to 3 hours, though a snack can certainly provide a nice break and an energy boost. On hikes longer than that, your body requires nourishment and starts sending that signal to you: You'll feel hungry. You might also feel fatigued or lethargic. Why? Consider these statistics: The average woman, when sedentary, burns 2100 calories a day, and a sedentary man burns around 2800 calories a day. That's without any exercise. Yet, according to the website *www.caloriesperhour.com,* a 35-year-old woman who is 5 feet, 5 inches tall and weighs 130 pounds that hikes uphill with a pack weighing 10 to 20 pounds will burn 1705 calories in just 4 hours. A man who is 5 feet, 9 inches tall and weighs 150 pounds that carries the same pack on the same hike will consume 2054 calories in 4 hours. Those numbers help illustrate that hiking is great exercise but also show that your body needs to replenish its energy stores on a hike of any duration.

Here's how it works. Your body converts everything you eat into three main energy sources: **protein, fats,** and **carbohydrates.** Of these, carbohydrates are the fuel of choice, because your body more easily uses them than fats or protein. In fact, your body breaks down carbohydrates almost instantly into a simple sugar called glucose, which supplies energy to your muscles, organs, and nervous system. Excess glucose in the blood is converted into glycogen, which is stored in your muscles and liver and is converted back into blood glucose when your body needs extra energy. You prevent fatigue by consuming enough calories, carbohydrates, and fluid.

How Much Should You Eat?

Given what you've read above about caloric needs on a hike and that most food packaging contains information about the amount of calories in the product, you can plan accordingly for your body and your hike. The highly respected National Outdoor Leadership School (NOLS) uses this rule of thumb for planning food for its program participants: 1.5 to 2 pounds of food provides 2500 to 3000 calories. If you're not interested in turning your hike preparation into a math exercise, just bring some energy-rich snacks on your hikes, and you'll soon figure out how much you'll feel you need to eat on a given hike.

What Should You Eat?

Widely accepted nutritional guidelines suggest that a healthy diet is 50 percent carbohydrates, 30 percent fats, and 20 percent proteins. Your body will tell you what it needs, and when you're active, your body will tend to crave more carbohydrates. On a hike, you'll want foods that travel well in a pack and don't need refrigeration. Foods fitting that description that are also high in carbohydrates include cereal, dried fruit, bagels or bread, fig bars, chocolate bars, snack bars, energy bars, and fresh vegetables that keep well, such as carrots. Fats contain about twice the calories per pound of carbohydrates or protein and provide the slow-burning fuel that keeps you moving long after your last meal or snack. Fats are found in cheese, chocolate, canned meat or fish, pepperoni, sausage, and nuts or nut products such as peanut butter. Proteins are necessary to cell health and are found in cheese, beans, nuts, and grains such as oatmeal, crackers, breads, and bagels.

Research also suggests that it's wise to eat at least a small meal in the 50-30-20 proportions of carbohydrates to fat to protein—such as a bagel with cream cheese—within 30 minutes to 2 hours after finishing a hike (or other workout). Just as importantly, what you eat the day before your hike influences your energy level while hiking. Plan your day-before-hiking "training table" considering those broad dietary guidelines—say, by having a dinner of pasta with a green vegetable and a piece of fruit for dessert—and you'll make your hike a more enjoyable experience.

Make your trail food something you look forward to eating. Plan for variety in texture and taste with raisins; nuts; crunchy foods such as nuts, crackers, and corn nuts; and chewy things such as dried fruit, fruit bars, and cheese. Fresh fruit and vegetables are a little heavier than dry food but a treat on a hot day hike; choose produce that holds up well, such as carrots, pears, oranges, and apples rather than bananas, grapes, and overripe peaches. Remember to pack out all produce waste such as rinds and peels.

Packing Food

Food can get hot and beat up in your pack. Choose foods that will survive some abuse, such as bagels instead of sliced bread. Put food in appropriate protective

A lightweight aluminum pot serves double duty as a salad bowl on the trail.

containers such as heavy-duty (or freezer) zipper-lock bags, plastic vacuum-sealed containers, refillable food tubes (for items such as peanut butter), or reusable food packaging such as a potato chip can. Storing all or most of your food in a nylon stuff sack keeps it together, offers enhanced protection from other objects in your pack, and keeps food from soiling clothing or other items inside your pack. Use clothing as padding to prevent crushing food. You can fashion a "refrigerator" of sorts inside your pack to preserve cheese, chocolate, and other things that suffer from heat by packing that food next to a cold water bottle and insulating everything with extra clothing (collapsible bottles and hydration bladders work better than hard plastic bottles; you could place the bottle inside a nylon food stuff sack). On a cool day, just the insulation of clothing in your pack will protect food from the sun's heat. Foods bought at supermarkets are encased in plastic and cardboard that add bulk and weight to your pack, so strip away excess packaging and put the food in the protective containers suggested earlier. You can also buy food in bulk and repackage it. Because food is one of the heaviest and densest items you're likely to carry, it should be packed at shoulder blade level or higher in your backpack and close to your back (see "Loading a Pack" in Chapter 2). Snack items go in outer pockets for easy access.

There are numerous books that offer advice on what foods to bring into the backcountry and how to prepare interesting and tasty treats (see Appendix B and *Backpacker* magazine).

Don't Feed the Animals!

You've seen those four words on signs in national parks and other public lands. Please take them to heart. Feeding human food to animals can make them ill and disrupt their normal eating and food-gathering habits. Training animals to spend their time begging food from people rather than finding their own actually reduces their long-term chances of survival. Some cute animals may also bite humans who are feeding them or humans who *refuse* to feed an animal that has been conditioned to expect handouts from previous contacts with people. Studies have found that when bears accustomed to human food are trained (through the use of stinging rubber bullets and other methods) to disassociate humans with food, it takes just *one* feeding incident out of twenty subsequent encounters with people for the animal to again associate people with food. Animals conditioned to receiving food from humans may become a threat to people and often are then destroyed by park managers.

Beyond even the question of deliberately feeding food to animals, you should be careful to prevent animals from getting into your food, for the same reasons. Some animals, including gray jays, raccoons, squirrels, mice, and bears, have grown accustomed to rummaging through hikers' packs for food, foraging on the ground around where hikers have eaten for crumbs and scraps. Keep an eye on your pack, and don't assume your food is protected inside just because the pack is closed—in fact, some animals chew through a pack, thus damaging it. Try not to drop food on the ground when you stop to eat.

Always pack out all trash and food scraps such as banana peels. If you want to make the backcountry a cleaner place for you having been there, pick up and carry out any trash you see.

Chapter 5

Children on the Trail

M y son Nate was 4 days old when my wife and I took him on his first hike—not 4 years old, 4 *days* old. By his first birthday, he'd been on five backpacking trips and an inestimable number of day hikes, ski tours, and camping trips in seven states and two Canadian provinces. As I write this, Nate is entering his second summer of life and we've already got big hiking plans for him this summer, including a visit to Yosemite right before his second birthday. We've already made the following adjustments to our hiking methodology to accommodate him as a toddler compared with hiking with him as an infant: (1) letting him start out on foot at the outset of a hike (although he covers pretty good distance by himself, he tends to travel in circles and not make much forward progress), (2) putting him in the kid carrier backpack only when he's ready for a break, (3) having snacks and juice readily available, and (4) choosing trails along creeks because he's fascinated by moving water.

We know we'll always have to plan our family hikes around Nate's abilities and interests—and just as we had to diligently watch him that first summer to keep him from putting dangerous things into his mouth, there will be safety concerns when we hike with him for years to come. We also already see his fascination with the outdoors—the scurrying of animals, the song of birds, the sound and motion of a creek—and we want more than anything to raise him with the same appreciation for the outdoors that my wife and I have.

Start children hiking young to develop a love for the outdoors. Here, the author's wife and son enjoy Idaho's Rapid Wild and Scenic River.

Having children doesn't mean you have to stop enjoying hiking or the outdoors. On the contrary, children give you more reasons to get out there. If you weren't a hiker before becoming a parent, children are a great reason to take up the activity: It's something everyone can do, at any age, inexpensively, that's healthy and an awful lot of fun. With a bit of know-how, some toys and games to entertain, and decent gear and clothing to keep your offspring warm and dry, exploring the backcountry becomes a fantastic family experience. Parents who've watched children grow up hiking will tell you they took great pleasure in seeing their kids grow in confidence, letting them lean on their trust in the parent until they trusted themselves enough to go it alone. Keep in mind the following tips on hiking with children of all ages.

General Tips for Hiking with Children

- ▲ **Choose an area kids will enjoy.** For young kids, a creek that's safe to play in is usually a big hit. For older kids, rocks they can scramble around on safely can distract them for hours.
- ▲ **Plan ahead and get input from the kids.** With ownership in a trip, children become enthused.
- ▲ **Start out small.** Whether you're carrying an infant or young child in a pack, or your child is hiking, begin with short hikes and gradually see how much farther your child is willing to go. Look for destinations where hikes of varying length are possible; that way, you can cut it short or go farther, depending on how things are going that particular day.
- ▲ **Start out simple.** Rocky, hilly trails are much harder on little legs than on adult legs. Be aware of the trail conditions and elevation gain and loss where you're going. Make sure your children are physically ready for the hike, or pick another one.

▲ **Bring baby wipes.** Use an unscented baby wipe to wash away grime before and after meals and to clean little hands after a potty break. Available in small and large plastic carriers, these always-ready washcloths are indispensable, especially in environments where water is scarce.

▲ **Upgrade the first-aid kit.** With kids in the picture, you'll need to adjust the contents of your first-aid kit. Bring children's acetaminophen or ibuprofen, aloe vera gel for soothing sunburn and other skin irritations, and stock up on twice as many adhesive bandages. Eyewash is also a good idea for twigs that slap kids in the face or mud that gets in the eye. A good pair of tweezers to pull out the inevitable splinters, cactus spines, and ticks is a must.

▲ **Have a "Plan B."** Research the access points and safety resources in the area you plan to hike, and program in the flexibility to go to a Plan B itinerary if things don't go exactly as planned.

▲ **Don't set an agenda.** Let the kids' energy level dictate how far you go. Keep it enjoyable for them rather than making it an unpleasant experience, and they'll want to go out again.

▲ **Provide food with kid appeal.** Feed children often. Fat-free newtons (such as fig, raspberry, or apple), animal crackers, dry cereal, hard cheese and crackers, dried fruit, and gorp all make good, high-energy snacks. Let your child pick the ingredients for the gorp. Avoid giving a child hard candy, nuts, and raw carrots; a child breathing heavily or excited could choke on these things.

▲ **Get good gear.** A comfortable kid carrier backpack can make the difference between whether you actually go out hiking or leave an uncomfortable pack in the storage room because you dread wearing it. Think about any hiking gear or clothing in the same way, including for your kids. No, that doesn't mean you have to spend a lot of money. (Haven't I said that enough yet?) However, if you and your kids are not comfortable, you won't be as happy—and you might be miserable. If outfitting your family with new stuff isn't in the budget, then simply choose hikes for which the clothing and gear you already own is adequate to keep you comfortable.

▲ **Avoid bug season.** Mixing kids and bugs is a recipe for misery.

▲ **Bring a comfort item.** Whatever the age of the child, bring along on your hike or camping trip a "comfort item" that could help calm or entertain the child. This might be a favorite blanket, stuffed animal, toy, or book.

Tips for Hiking with Infants to Children Age 2

▲ **Watch the head.** As soon as baby can hold her head up, you have the green light to hit the trail. Load her in a chest carrier, which allows you to shoulder a light pack, as well. When a baby's weight gets up around fifteen to twenty pounds, you'll find her too heavy for the chest carrier and will want to switch to a child-carrier backpack.

Kids need the right clothing just like adults—use layers to protect a child from cold and wind.

▲ **Pack food kids like.** Nursing infants need only Mama for food. Bring dried banana strips (not slices) for teething toddlers; they keep infants busy for long stretches of time, if you don't mind the drool. Bring a hand-crank food mill for grinding up the leftovers from adult meals to feed babies who eat some solid foods.

▲ **Childproof the hike.** When baby is in the put-everything-in-his-or-her-mouth stage, seek out hiking destinations with chokeproof terrain, such as a sandy beach or grassy meadow, and watch her like a hawk.

▲ **Ride in style.** Decorate your child carrier with dangling playpen doodads to make it more like home.

▲ **Watch out.** When your child is in a child-carrier pack on your back, a small mirror in your pocket will let you look at your baby to see how he's doing without having to take your pack off (although having a second adult along to help deal with little things, such as wiping a nose, is more convenient). Also, have a towel or fleece to arrange as a pillow for your infant or toddler when he falls asleep back there, so his head isn't hanging off to one side (which may be more uncomfortable for you than for him).

▲ **Keep the piggies warm.** Bundle little feet in insulated booties during cool hikes. Lack of movement, combined with restricted circulation in legs dangling from the carrier cockpit, can lead to cold piggies and irritability.

Tips for Hiking with Children Ages 2 to 6

▲ **Bribe with trail treats.** Diversions of the edible variety are an essential hiking tool. Bring trail mix, gummy worms, lollipops, or licorice. Set goals for the next treat stop: a mile, half an hour, the next lake, a huge tree in the distance.

▲ **Plan playtime.** Schedule numerous rest and play stops. Kids tire faster than adults do, plus they can teach you a thing or two about stopping to smell the flowers.

▲ **Walk with wheels.** On well-groomed trails, a jogging stroller allows you to carry a full pack and still ferry your child when she becomes too tired to walk. NOTE: You can't take jogging strollers into designated wilderness areas, where wheeled vehicles are prohibited.

▲ **Think quality, not quantity.** A successful family hike doesn't have to cover much ground if there are rocks to scramble on, trees to climb, and water to play in. Adults tend to have a "proceed from Point A to Point B" mentality, but kids are much more likely to be satisfied with immediate experiences. Keep your mileage well below what you would cover without children.

▲ **Let them get dirty.** Parents who are fanatics about regularly bathing their children must check that notion at the trailhead.

▲ **Plan to hike along a stream or near a lake.** There's nothing like sand, mud, and water to occupy or cheer up children.

▲ **"Smellproof" the hike.** Reduce your child's attractiveness to animals and insects by avoiding sweet-smelling lotions and wipes.

▲ **Occupy their minds.** Encourage kids to chat about things to keep their minds off hiking. Start a story line and pass it from person to person, or try participatory camp songs (think "Itsy Bitsy Spider").

▲ **Keep them busy.** Distract an unhappy toddler with a game involving something seen along the trail or something as simple as kicking a stone down the trail.

For young children, hiking is a great adventure. Let them take turns leading the hike, but keep an eye them.

Tips for Hiking with Children Ages 6 to 12

▲ **Think "the more, the merrier."** Bring friends or hook up with other families. The kids entertain each other, plus parents can take turns watching the crew and getting some much-needed adult time.

▲ **Snap away.** Give kids a disposable or inexpensive camera so they can chronicle their expedition.

▲ **Go fish.** A simple spin-casting rig and a few lures can entertain for many an afternoon. Be prepared to do some wading for the inevitable snagged hooks.

▲ **Let them lead.** Let kids lead, especially when they begin to lag behind. Sometimes putting them up front and giving them the power to dictate the pace translates into a burst of energy.

▲ **Gear up for less.** When money is an object, spend your pennies on top-of-the-line long underwear, shell wear, and footwear. Skimp on no-name fleece.

▲ **Capture the wild in words.** Bring journals for the youngsters to write and color in. Have them trace leaves and sketch salamanders to create long-lasting memories.

▲ **Be prepared.** Bring one more set of clothes than you think you need for your child. Kids always get wetter and muddier than you expect.

▲ **Don't weigh them down.** Don't overload kids with pack weight. Let a child who's old enough carry a pack, but its weight should be dictated by the child's size and ability.

Tips for Hiking with Children Ages 12 to 18

▲ **Let the big kids hike ahead.** Teenagers have more energy than you do and need personal space. If it's safe, allow them to hike at their own pace. Use trail junctions, water crossings, and other landmarks for meeting points. Bring a buddy. A teen who takes a friend along has a good shot at having fun.

▲ **Fuel the flock.** Growing teenagers—especially boys—need to eat a lot and often. Stuff their pockets with trail mix and energy bars so you don't have a feeding frenzy at every meal.

▲ **Teach, don't do.** Kids age 12 and older are ready to learn hiking skills. Teach them how to use a compass, load and adjust their pack, and so on.

▲ **Plan a lot of free time.** Physically, teens may be capable of hiking all day, but that doesn't mean it's good for them. Throw in a deck of cards, Hacky Sack, or Frisbee. Bring a field book and make a contest out of identifying plants. Allow time to swim, have snowball fights, write in journals, and sketch.

▲ **Don't skimp on gear.** Many teens are able to carry an adult-size load, and it's unfair to ask them to do it with a child-size pack. In general, buy them adult products that are durable and adjustable in fit. You'll save money in the long run if big-ticket items like packs don't have to be replaced again. On the other hand, their feet grow fast, so don't invest a lot of money in top-of-the-line boots that will be two sizes too small by the time they're broken in. For three-season hiking, choose lightweight footwear with adequate ankle support. If you plan on-trail hikes only, durable sneakers may be adequate.

▲ **Lead by example.** It won't be long before these kids will be hiking on their own. It's up to you to teach them low-impact techniques and respect for the wilderness.

▲ **Share closets.** Teens can wear the same clothing you do. Perfect fit and costly technical features aren't necessary, but it's important that layers keep your teen warm and dry.

Nutrition and Hydration

See, those words always look more serious than "food and water." It's perhaps more critical with children than with adults to keep the fluids and food coming, because the small bodies of young children need to replenish their energy reserves more frequently, and teenagers, especially boys, have ravenous appetites (as a parent of a teen knows) and need it satisfied when they're exerting themselves. If your child doesn't like water, bring juice or a powdered drink she will like. If your young child will carry her own water bottle, let her; she'll feel a sense of participation and responsibility. Make sure the water bottle you give your child is one he can handle and drink from easily. Older children can certainly carry their own food, water, and clothing. Also, make sure young children know not to drink from streams and other backcountry water sources.

Sun Protection

Whether your children are hiking with you or playing out in your yard, consider this statistic: 80 percent of skin damage from the sun, including skin cancers, happens before age 20, although it usually doesn't show up for 30 years. It's vitally important to protect kids from the sun. Dress them in tightly woven clothing and use sunscreen on all uncovered skin. Infants should be kept out of the sun, but avoid using sunscreen on them unless it's necessary, and start by applying a little sunscreen to a small area of the baby's skin to see whether the baby has a reaction to it. If a child gets sunburned, immediately apply cold compresses and moisturizing lotion and give the child acetaminophen for the pain. Try to convince your children to wear sunglasses to protect their sensitive eyelids and to reduce the chance of cataracts later in life.

Kids vs. Bugs and Animals

As suggested earlier, it's best to maintain a distance between kids and bugs and animals. However, it's not always possible to avoid biting insects. If bugs are bugging your kids, the first line of defense is clothing that covers them—which doubles as good protection against ultraviolet (UV) rays from the sun, a particular threat to young skin. Think in terms of long-sleeve shirts, pants rather than shorts, tall hiking socks, a hat with a wide brim or a bill and a sun shade that covers the back of the neck and ears, and perhaps even mosquito netting to drape over the hat. If the weather is warm, make sure their clothing is lightweight, cool, and breathes well, otherwise hard-working kids are going to get too hot.

The Bugs

If you want to use a bug repellent, get one made for kids or one made with natural ingredients rather than chemicals. The chemical **deet** is the active ingredient in many bug repellents. Some products with less than 15 percent deet have been advertised as safe for use on children. According to the Environmental Protection Agency, there's no scientific data to support such an assertion, which is one of the reasons the agency no longer allows child-safety claims on deet products. Still, let the buyer beware. Some stores may continue to sell deet products that claim to be safe for children, based on a formula that involves manufacture and distribution dates. Children have much more surface area relative to their body mass, which puts them at risk for dangerous levels of deet absorption. Some experts recommend that no formula containing more than 10 percent deet be used on children. Experts recommend avoiding sunscreen/repellent all-in-one lotions, because sunscreen should be reapplied often but repellent should not. Finally, always wash off any deet-based repellent with soap and water before bedtime to avoid unnecessary accumulation of the chemical. Keep chemical bug repellents off of children's hands to avoid the chemical getting into their eyes and mouths.

The Animals

Children of all ages get excited by and attracted to animals, which can be good and bad. Start teaching children as soon as they can understand how to identify animals that they should avoid them or admire them from afar. Animals that are habituated to receiving food from people may approach you or your child, and sometimes even the cutest little critters can get aggressive and bite. Don't encourage your child to feed or pet a wild animal (see Chapter 4); you can endanger your child.

Most large animals do not prey upon humans, even children, but there are areas of the country where predators are a concern. **Mountain lions** live in much of the West and in rare instances have been known to prey upon children and small adults. Be aware of whether you're in mountain lion country, and keep children close by. If you encounter a lion, group closely together and make a lot of noise and wave your arms; try to scare it off, and don't turn your back on it. Mountain lions hunt by stalking and pouncing upon their prey from behind, and a lion isn't believed likely to approach a party that's acting aggressively toward it.

Grizzly bears still roam select areas of the Northern Rockies, including Glacier, Yellowstone, and Grand Teton National Parks and some neighboring national forests. Thousands of visitors day-hike and backpack in these parks and forests every year without problems; still, grizzlies should always be considered dangerous. If you see one, leave the area immediately. The national parks provide plenty of information on how to avoid and deal with grizzly encounters; bone up on it before you go hiking. Generally, it's wise in grizzly country to stick to established trails, hike in a group, stay together, make plenty of noise, and avoid carrying smelly foods such as canned fish.

Black bears are much more prevalent, living in most wooded and mountainous areas of the country. They are much more docile than grizzlies and often avoid people, but those that have gotten food from humans in the past usually try to do it again and may get aggressive. If a black bear approaches you, shout at it, wave your arms, bang loud things together such as cook pots, and throw rocks at the bear until it goes away. Never approach a black bear, and don't let your kids do anything to provoke it. Watching a black bear from a distance is often safe as long as your presence does not appear to be affecting the bear's behavior. If the bear reacts to you, leave the area.

Daylight hours are safest for avoiding animal encounters, and predawn and dusk are the times you're most likely to see wildlife. You might want to take advantage of early morning and evening to view elk, moose, or other animals that pose little or no threat, but avoid these hours—or simply be hyper-alert—if big predators such as grizzlies or mountain lions are about. And keep the kids close by.

Chapter 6

Safety, Fun, and Trail Ethics

his book's first chapter suggested that you could go hiking without reading any further. Hopefully, you've at least done some easier hikes now and realize that, at a basic level, hiking really is nothing more than putting one foot in front of the other. Of course, you also know that it can get a little more complicated than that, too. Unlike walking down a sidewalk, on the trail we have to pay closer attention to where we're going to avoid getting lost or confused—or tripping and falling. When we're outdoors and far from civilization, we must be aware of the consequences of our decisions and of the injuries that can happen in an environment that, unlike civilization, has not been manipulated to maximize our comfort and safety. We're usually sharing the trail with other people and should consider how our behavior might affect their experience (just as we hope they will reciprocate that courtesy). We should also consider our physical impact on the trail and surrounding natural world, including wildlife.

If this sounds too complicated, rest assured that all of these things will come naturally to you if you simply keep them in the back of your mind, ready to pull to the forefront of your thoughts when the time comes. As I've said in earlier chapters, the objective of this book is to take you as far as you want to go into hiking and to teach you as much as you feel you want or need to learn. If you stick to your small,

This remote-looking scene is actually on a popular hike in Maine's Acadia National Park. All hikers should do their part to minimize their impact on trails and natural resources.

local state park or forest, where trails are wide and groomed and intersections are clearly marked with signs or maps, you may never need to summon any skill more advanced than your innate common sense. But if you've read this far, you're probably interested in (1) learning more about hiking, (2) learning what you need to know to venture out on longer day hikes in the mountains and forests, and (3) learning how to recognize which hikes demand more advanced skills and which do not. This chapter delves into a range of skills for hiking trails, some very fundamental, others more advanced and suited to specific circumstances. Read on as much as you'd like, then put the book down. Later, when you're ready, you'll pick it up again to learn something new. In the meantime, don't forget why you're reading this book: Keep on hiking and developing your skills in real-life situations while having fun.

At the Trailhead

With so much of this book's focus on prehike planning and what to do on the trail, it's easy to overlook the trailhead itself, that buffer zone between civilization and wilderness. It's a bit of a cross between both worlds, and for your own benefit, you have to think of it as just that.

Know the Road to the Trailhead

First of all, don't assume a good road to the trailhead. Yes, some trailheads are reached by paved or good gravel roads that are easily traveled by car. Other trailheads lie at the end of miles of rough road only navigable by high-clearance, four-wheel-drive or all-wheel-drive vehicles. Some roads are navigable by any vehicle when dry, yet completely impassable to any vehicle when wet. Find out about the road to the trailhead where you plan to hike, its current condition, and the potential for its condition to worsen (usually as a result of foul weather) while you're parked there and on your hike. Make sure your vehicle can handle the road; if it can't, rent or borrow a vehicle that can make it or choose another hike. Nothing will ruin an outing like getting stranded on a remote road before you even reach the trailhead, or after the hike, on the drive out.

Be Alert When Driving to the Trailhead

We tend to concentrate on safety during our hike, yet too often turn off our safety radar while driving to the trailhead, which is often the most dangerous part of a hike. If you're hiking in a rural area, one of the greatest dangers is a large animal such as a deer, moose, or antelope dashing out in front of your moving vehicle and colliding, often causing serious damage to the vehicle and injuring or killing its occupants—not to mention the animal. When driving in the dark or during the evening or early-morning hours (when light is dim and animals are active), slow down and stay alert. Don't drive if you're too tired, particularly after a strenuous hike.

Plan to Stay the Night

I almost always keep extra food, water or other beverage, and a change of clothing in my car's trunk just in case I'm in desperate need of them when I return to the car, or—as can happen in remote areas with marginal roads—just in case I'm unable to drive away from the trailhead after the hike.

Don't Trespass

Some trailheads lie on or adjacent to private land, and hiking access may be at the discretion of the landowner. Access is always at risk when a trail or trailhead sits on private land, and it's up to every hiker who uses it to help maintain public access by respecting the rights of the property owner. Don't trespass where you don't belong. Don't leave trash or anything else behind. Obey any posted signs. It's a matter of preserving public access and simple courtesy.

Be Prepared for Crime

One sad reality about hiking is that the trailhead lies within reach of civilization's less-proud elements, and crime does occasionally occur. Predominantly, this takes the form of theft and vandalism to cars parked at trailheads. This shouldn't deter you from hiking any more than concern about theft would deter you from parking your car in an urban area when you go to dinner. However, you should be aware of the possibility and act accordingly to minimize your risk. The following is advice concerning trailhead security; many of these tips are subjective and you ultimately have to make the judgment as to what's the best strategy for your situation.

▲ Choose popular or very remote hikes. The riskiest trailheads are the ones that receive moderate use (six or seven cars), and those that are on or close to a main road. Trailheads with many people coming and going are safer, as are those that are difficult to reach.

▲ Look around the parking lot for evidence of break-ins, such as broken automobile glass on the ground.

▲ Make your vehicle ugly. Some hikers—myself included—insist that an old, dirty vehicle is less attractive to thieves than a new, clean vehicle. If you have to leave possessions visible in your vehicle, consider making any of the following most visible: empty beer cans, spent shotgun shells, trash, and (my personal favorite tactic) dirty underwear.

▲ If your car is empty, leave it unlocked to let thieves discover, without having to break in, that there's nothing to steal. On the other hand, unlocked doors do provide easier access to vandals striking randomly. If the doors are locked and the car empty, leave the glove compartment empty and open.

▲ Leave your wallet or purse at home. Carry the cash you need and any credit or calling cards in your pack.

▲ Install a removable car stereo and leave it anywhere but in the vehicle while you're hiking.

▲ Never leave coins in plain view.

▲ Install a car alarm and display stickers advising thieves of its presence.

▲ Never trust your trunk as a safe storage area for anything.

▲ Use an antitheft device if your vehicle model is one that is stolen frequently.

▲ Check with the public lands manager about the incidence of crime at the trailhead you intend to visit.

▲ Make sure your automobile insurance covers theft and vandalism.

▲ Report any thefts that you do suffer so that authorities are encouraged to address the problem through enforcement.

▲ Be aware of other people at the trailhead. If they don't look like backpackers or hikers, they may not be. Write down the license plate number of suspicious individuals.

▲ Park your car near other vehicles where a higher level of human traffic may deter thieves.

▲ If hiking in an urban park, complete your hike before dark.

▲ If there are several cars in your party, pile everyone into one vehicle for the last few miles and leave the other vehicles at a safe spot.

▲ Use a shuttle service to reach the trailhead if possible.

▲ If you're in an area where an environmental dispute is raging, such as the timberlands of the Northwest, consider temporarily removing any bumper sticker or decal that shows your support for conservation organizations, so that you're not a target for thieves or vandals.

Trail Etiquette

The woods and mountains are not the sort of places where people generally worry about rules of social conduct. But the truth is, many of us share the trails, especially popular, scenic hikes near population centers. To keep everyone smiling, friendly, and happy, a modicum of decorum is in order. It takes so little effort to extend simple courtesies to one another and makes the trail such a nicer place.

Monitor Your Noise Level

For starters, be aware of your noise level and think of others around you. On some popular hikes there are so many people that your boisterous conversation or shouts could hardly matter; ditto on remote trails when you know there's no one around—who would you bother with your noise?! But we're often on hikes where other people are close by, well within earshot, yet there aren't so many folks that the din of conversation rises to a cacophony. When only a few small groups of hikers share a summit or other spot along the trail, things tend to remain pretty quiet, as

Popular summits can get crowded, so all hikers should respect others by keeping noise to a minimum and dispersing.

each group presumes the others would prefer to enjoy the quietude of nature rather than overhear their conversation. This is as it should be, so be cognizant of your own noise level when you're in that type of situation.

Turn Off the Cellular Phone

I mentioned cellular telephones in Chapter 2, but the etiquette of using them in the backcountry is worth discussing again here. Many hikers find it offensive to see or hear someone speaking on a cellular phone in a pristine place; they feel they have come to the wilderness precisely to get away from such manifestations of civilization. Unless we all respect the highest ethic about keeping the backcountry free of the clutter and baggage of the "real world," we'll wind up with a lowest common denominator ethic governing what's acceptable, and that scenario may rob the backcountry of much of its appeal. If you feel it wise to carry a cellular phone in case of an emergency, then keep it stored out of sight and sound in your pack until an emergency arises. Don't make social calls around other people. Don't assume you'll even get a cellular signal—in most backcountry areas, especially in steep terrain, you won't. Don't think of a cellular phone as a substitute for good judgment or any other piece of emergency gear. In addition, don't leap to the conclusion that you need the help of rescuers: In most backcountry situations, help wouldn't arrive for hours, anyway, so take the time to analyze your situation and verify whether your party can help itself or actually does require help. Since the proliferation of cellular phones in the backcountry, rescuers have many times been called to a scene by hikers who panicked and immediately used the cellular phone, only to arrive and be told by the hikers that they didn't require a rescue after all.

Share the Trail

Depending on where you're hiking, you might find yourself sharing the trail with many other types of users who are there legally, just like you. Other trail users can include horseback riders, mountain bikers, hunters, skiers, and snowmobilers. Sometimes members of different user groups show animosity toward one another, when in reality everyone shares an equal privilege to be there. Whatever you may feel about someone else's activity of choice, doing something to foment ill will only puts other hikers and trail users at risk of suffering some reciprocation of that ill will later. If you don't want to run into nonhikers, then stick to trails that only permit hikers; there are plenty of them. Otherwise, accept that we live in a society where people have different ways of enjoying the backcountry.

Finding Your Way

Imagine this scenario: You and a companion are strolling along a trail in the woods, talking at length and focusing more on your conversation than on where you're going. Suddenly, without apparent warning, the trail appears to terminate, just like that. Ahead of you lies only thick forest, with no path parting it. You turn around and realize for the first time that the trail you were following doesn't look as wide and well groomed here as it had for most of your hike; in fact, it's fairly narrow and nearly overgrown with brush. You look around and see no trail markers, no signs, no other people, although you'd passed plenty of other hikers earlier. It occurs to you that you're not sure how far you've walked, how long you've been hiking, or exactly where you are. A profound and somewhat disturbing feeling of disorientation overwhelms you, and you wonder: How did this happen?

Actually, it happens easily and frequently—to both novices and experienced hikers who make the same mistake of not paying close enough attention to where their feet are taking them. If you retrace your steps—as you probably would naturally do—you're likely to discover that you had left the real trail a short distance back, at a bend in the trail that looks obvious to you now but that you'd somehow overlooked and walked straight past. The false path you'd walked onto without breaking stride exists because so many hikers before you had made the same mistake, and the cumulative impact of their boots had trampled out this "rogue path." The rogue path dissipates quickly because the first few hikers who made that mistake only walked a short distance off-trail before realizing their blunder, and most of the errant hikers who followed pulled up abruptly, as you did, when the trail appeared to suddenly terminate.

The lesson? Even on a popular, well-marked and well-maintained trail, you can take a wrong turn for no better reason than not paying attention. However, on a hike such as that, finding your way requires little more than simply staying on your toes. Watch the trail and its markers, and don't overlook bends in the path. Keep track of how long you've been hiking, and estimate how far you've gone based on your hiking pace (which you'll learn to gauge through practice) and landmarks such as obvious terrain features or trail junctions. By doing that, you'll avoid wasting energy going the wrong way, potentially getting lost for a long period, and damaging the forest by creating a rogue path that gets trampled into existence by distracted hikers.

Trail Maps

The first and most basic tool for finding your way on a hike is a trail map. Virtually anywhere that you hike, you should carry a map of the area—unless, as in some city and state parks, maps are available at trail junctions or signs clearly indicate where you are and the direction to walk to reach various destinations. We've all used road maps; reading a trail map is much like reading a road map, except that they offer different information because they're made for different uses. A road map shows roads and cities, states, and points of interest found along roads. A trail map shows roads in the area, of course, but its focus is the area's trails and points of interest along them, such as public lands boundaries, ranger stations, campsites, huts, waterfalls, peaks, viewpoints, rivers, lakes, and streams. Nonetheless, you read them both the same way: If you're following a trail and you know your direction of travel on the map, then you'll know whether to turn right or left at a key intersection to continue toward your destination.

Like a road map, the trail map has a distance scale you can use to calculate how far you've gone or have yet to go, usually in both miles and kilometers, and it shows alternate routes available. The scale is generally indicated on a map with a ratio like 1:66,667, which means that 1 inch on the map equals 66,667 inches on the ground. While that information may seem useless to a novice map user, once you grow accustomed to using maps of differing scales, you'll develop a sense for what kind of detail a map can provide based on its scale.

Consult your map frequently enough to maintain a sense of your location, both to avoid inadvertently missing a turn or trail junction and to more easily reorient yourself if you get "temporarily lost" (see more on that below).

There are different kinds of trail maps out there. Some—as you might find at a small state park—show only an approximate representation of the trail system and trailheads in the place where you're hiking, without other details such as the land and water features present there. Some rudimentary maps don't even always have the area in the correct scale—that is, distances between points (such as trail junctions) on the map do not provide an accurate representation of the true distances between those points on the ground. Such basic maps may be adequate for finding your way through a small park that has well-marked trails, where you really can't get very lost. However, if you're striking off on a longer hike, especially into rugged terrain with a lot of ups and downs, you'll want what is called a **topographical,** or **topo map**. Topo maps are distinguished by a network of contour lines covering the map, those squiggly lines that indicate elevation above sea level and the lay of the land.

To begin understanding how to read a topo map, you first have to know how to **orient** it—or simply put, to hold the map so that the direction north on the map faces north.

Using a Map and Compass

On good, easy-to-follow trails, you may never need a compass. But take a wrong turn, wander accidentally off the trail, or get turned around and disoriented, and having a compass could mean the difference between immediately getting back on track or wandering around aimlessly for hours. Besides, it's inexpensive, small, and lightweight, so there's no reason for any hiker to not carry one.

Finding your way by using a compass with your map is a skill you can develop on many levels, as you see the need. That need depends largely on the difficulty of the trails you hike. To illustrate this point, let's revisit our hypothetical hikers of previous chapters, Cher, Elvis, and Madonna.

Scenario 1: Sticking to her popular, well-marked trails, Cher has never had to pull out the simple compass she bought when she first outfitted herself with boots and a pack—until the day of the fog. Hiking with a friend up a peak she's done several times, Cher reaches the summit and, as usual, goes to her favorite spot to sit and enjoy a snack and the view. As she and her friend relax under a warm sun, the wind suddenly stirs. Before they realize it, a low cloud has moved in front of the sun. Then, without warning, the cloud drops right onto their summit. Cher and her friend quickly pull on their jackets, pack up lunch, and turn to hike down. But in the thick fog, they get turned around and can't figure out which direction their trail lies. They can't see more than several feet, and the terrain looks the same in every direction: rocks. Instead of walking aimlessly, Cher produces the compass that's always in a side pocket of her pack. She uses it to orient her map, sees on the map that their trail descends off the west side of the summit, and uses the compass to lead them to the west—where they find trail markers. Minutes later, they're back in the woods, below the fog, easily following that familiar trail back to their car.

Scenario 2: Elvis decides he's ready to explore some national parks. He takes a vacation to the canyon parks of the southern Utah desert to day-hike and camp. These parks are staffed with helpful, competent rangers who are willing to help him select hikes, and there are good maps available. Still, he sees in the stark, almost treeless landscape that trails are not always obvious, and rogue paths created by hikers taking wrong turns never disappear in this dry environment. Elvis realizes that if he's not attentive to where he's going, he could take a wrong turn and quickly become lost. But he watches carefully for trail markers and cairns and the occasional trail signs. A few times, when he reaches a spot where he's not certain which direction to head, he pulls out his map and compass. Elvis uses his compass to orient his map and to determine his approximate location based on how far he estimates he's walked from the trailhead and on identifying prominent land features within sight that appear on his map. Within moments, he sees on the map the direction he should be walking and continues on his way.

Scenario 3: Madonna receives an invitation from a friend that really excites her—to join a group of people putting together a team to enter into an "adventure race." In these events, which are held all over the country and vary in how they're structured, teams of four people race through an outdoor course that involves finding their way through a landscape that isn't marked by trails or signs—in other words, navigating entirely with a map and compass. Before the race, Madonna takes a course in orienteering, learning fairly advanced map-and-compass skills, and finds herself enthralled by it. On race day, she emerges as the most adept member of her team at finding her way through dense forest using only the map and compass. Thanks to her, their team finishes third in a large and very competitive field.

As Cher, Elvis, and Madonna illustrate, there are many situations in which you might need a compass and many levels at which you can develop the skill of navigating through backcountry by map and compass. The following section explains first the fundamentals of compass use and then progresses into more advanced skills for those of you who think you'll need them.

What's the minimum you should know for hiking on good trails? If there was a course called Map and Compass Skills 101, it would teach you how to "orient" a map and determine your direction of travel using a compass. Orienting your map simply means turning it so that its arrow showing the direction of true north on the map points in that actual direction. Doing so aligns the map so that terrain features depicted on it lie in the same direction relative to your position on the map as those features actually lie in relation to where you're standing. In other words, if as you hold the map it shows a cliff to your right, you should be able to look in that direction and see that cliff (unless it is obstructed by something else). Being able to do this will not only help you find your way but also help you develop a better natural sense of your whereabouts and boost your confidence in your hiking skills. Knowing how to do this also informs you of the compass direction in which you're headed, and it brings the enjoyment of being able to identify prominent peaks, lakes, and other features.

The magnetic needle has an end that is red or orange, which always points to magnetic north, and an end that is white or black.

The rotating, circular faceplate—sometimes called a **graduated dial** or **rotating graduated dial**—is marked off in degrees. Markings also indicate the four basic compass points—north, east, south, and west—which correspond, respectively, with 0°/360°, 90°, 180°, and 270°. The faceplate also has one or more lines with direction arrows, known as **north-south lines.**

The compass base plate does not rotate. It also has at least one line called the **direction arrow** because you often walk in the direction it points when navigating with a compass.

Before trying to orient your map, set the map aside and use your compass to locate the four main compass directions. To do that, you must understand the term **declination** and the difference between true north and magnetic north. True north is where Santa Claus lives: the North Pole. Magnetic north is the Earth's magnetic north pole, determined by the planet's magnetic field, which is located in Arctic Canada south of the North Pole. Because a magnetized compass needle points to magnetic north rather than true north, to orient a map and know in what compass direction you're walking, you must know the declination where you are—that is, how great an angle east or west of true north that magnetic north lies relative to wherever you're standing. Declination is measured in degrees on a circle (which is 360°). For example, the declination in Yellowstone National Park is 15° east, meaning that magnetic north lies 15° degrees east of true north in that area.

The declination varies for different regions and is indicated on any good map.

This hiker uses a map and compass to determine his location and the direction he's heading.

So you don't actually have to calculate declination—merely check your map for it, then correct your compass for it. If you're in Yellowstone, to use our recent example, where the declination is 15° east, correct your compass for declination by rotating the round faceplate dial—which is marked off in degrees—so that the small arrow or line (that doesn't move) above the faceplate dial points to 15° east of north (north is 0° or 360°) on the dial. With the compass now corrected for declination, while holding it flat in your hand, turn yourself until the colored end (often orange or red) of the magnetic compass needle sits squarely inside the **faceplate arrow** (or two parallel colored lines on some compasses). As long as you keep the colored end of the needle inside the faceplate arrow, north on the dial points to true north, east points east, south points south, and west points west. You can walk in any direction and know the compass direction and degree bearing (for instance, east is 90°, west is 270°, southwest is 225°, etc.) in which you're headed.

Orienting a map is simple but easier to visualize if you use a map and compass while reading these instructions. Spread the map out flat. Lay your compass on the map and hold it in place. Set the rotating faceplate dial at 0°/360° (when you do this, the north-south lines of the faceplate point in the same direction as the base plate's direction arrow). Align the compass base plate direction arrow with the line indicating magnetic north on the map. Then rotate the compass and map together until the needle's colored end sits inside the faceplate arrow. Your map is now oriented, and any landscape feature within sight can be identified because its actual direction in relation to you corresponds with its direction from your position on the map. (Here's a friendly tip: Carry a plastic, zipper-lock bag in which you can put your map, folded so that the area of your hike faces up, to read in the rain.)

Note the compass direction in which your trail goes; discuss it aloud with your companions. For instance, you may start out heading southeast, then swing around to the south and eventually southwest, then turn sharply north to loop back to your starting point. Identify on the map various points along your hiking route, and note the direction from those points to important locations, such as the trailhead parking lot where your car sits. Identify alternative trails you might take if there arises a need to shorten your hike and get back to your car sooner. Refer back to the section in Chapter 1 called "How Hard Is *Hard*?" to estimate how long your hike will take.

Just as you're wise to try out a new pair of hiking boots by walking a few miles around town before taking them on the trail, you might also practice your map-and-compass skills around town before putting them to the test in the backcountry—maybe even while breaking in those new boots. These are skills worth developing. Many hiking clubs (see Appendix A) and stores that sell outdoor gear sponsor regular workshops on navigating with a map and compass, which are often inexpensive or free. Understanding your position and direction of travel helps develop your innate sense of orientation and direction, which will come in handy as you go on longer, more ambitious hikes.

Reading Between the Contour Lines

Once you can orient a topo map and see where your trails will take you, try reading its contour lines to "see" the terrain as represented on the flat map. Contour lines connect points that lie at the same elevation. Elevations are marked for some contour lines on a map, in feet or meters, and the map legend indicates what the constant interval is between all adjacent contour lines so that you can figure out the elevation of any point on any contour line. You can also simply look at two contour lines whose elevation is marked (these are usually more bold than the unmarked lines) and count the unmarked lines separating them. There are often four unmarked contour lines separating consecutive marked, bold lines. If the difference in elevation between the consecutive bold lines is 200 feet, then simple math reveals that each unmarked line between the bold contours represents 40 feet higher or lower elevation, depending on whether you're tracking uphill or downhill on the map. You can tell which direction is uphill or downhill on the map by reading the elevations at the marked contour lines. Topo maps also occasionally show shaded relief, that is, some areas are shaded on the map just as they would be by terrain with the sun casting shadows from a low point in the sky. The purpose of shaded relief is to give you a sense of the lay of the land.

Although a topographical map can appear confusing at first glance, they're easy to learn to read once you spend a few minutes studying one. Until you become familiar with using these maps, it's a good idea to spend a little time at home studying the map you'll use on an upcoming hike before you hit the trail.

Contour lines are useful for many reasons. They indicate how high you are and let you calculate precisely how much uphill and downhill, measurable in feet or meters, your hike entails. You can also pinpoint your location on a map when you reach an obvious feature, such as a trail junction or a viewpoint that's labeled on the map, and figure out how much more elevation you have to climb to reach a summit. Contour lines show a trail's steepness: The more spread out the contour lines, the gentler the terrain; the closer together the contour lines, the steeper the terrain. Relatively flat areas appear as broad gaps between contour lines. Of course, the ability of contour lines to show detail in the terrain is limited by the interval of the contours—that is, if the contour interval is 40 feet, then rolling terrain that doesn't vary by more than 40 feet in elevation appears on the map as blank (flat) area between widely spaced contours.

As your skill at reading a topo map improves, you'll be able to look at one and "read" the terrain to help determine where you are on the map. Reading the terrain around you and identifying it on your map usually requires two preconditions:

1. Your map shows sufficient detail, with contour lines indicating elevation gradations fairly close together, perhaps as little as 40 feet apart or less.
2. You have an approximate idea of your location, based on known information such as where you started your hike, roughly how far you've traveled, and in which direction on which trail.

Given this, look around and then peruse your map. Does that cliff off to your right appear on the map (probably as several contour lines packed together)? How about the deep gully off to your left? If you're on a trail, and your map shows a trail

Guide to Geographic Features in Topo Maps

Tarn	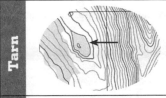	**Tarns** are small, steep-sided mountain pools.
Pass	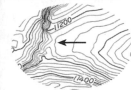	A **pass** is a narrow gap between mountain peaks, represented by two closed loops that approach each other but don't quite touch.
Butte	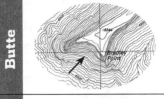	A **butte** is an isolated mountain that's flat-topped, or nearly so, and steep-walled.
Cirque	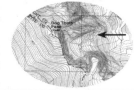	A **cirque** is a steep-sided bowl at the head of a glacier or stream. Contours will resemble an amphitheater.
Ridge	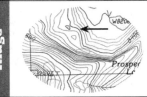	**Ridges** are shaped like Vs or Us; the contours point toward lower ground.
Canyon	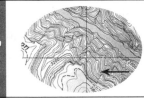	**Canyons** are deep, narrow valleys with steep sides, distinguished from ravines by a higher elevation profile and usually the presence of a stream.
Ravine	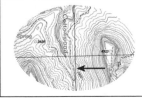	A **ravine** is deep and narrow and smaller than a canyon. V-shaped contour lines point toward higher ground and the elevation profile is generally 200 feet or less.

(Courtesy *Backpacker* magazine)

passing between those two features, you might be able to pinpoint your location. If you've lost your trail and can similarly identify nearby terrain features, you might use them and your map to find your way back to the trail or at least figure out the general direction you must walk to run into the trail.

You'll notice another detail about a good topo map that you may or may not use. Along the map's edges are markings that indicate the nearest whole-number lines of longitude and latitude for that area, measured in degrees and subdivided incrementally by minutes, with 60 minutes to each degree of longitude or latitude. These numbers come in handy when you're trying to establish your position on the map using a Global Positioning System (GPS) receiver (see "Global Positioning System" below), for instance, or when trying to align two maps that cover adjacent areas.

Taking a Compass Bearing

A more advanced skill involves using a map and compass to find your way from one point to another, or through a series of points along a route. This may be necessary when hiking off-trail or, for instance, if you find yourself in a thick fog on a treeless mountaintop with visibility so limited that you can't distinguish trail markers or remember in which direction you're supposed to hike (as Cher experienced in Scenario 1).

To plot a course on a map and reach that place using your compass, lay the compass on the map with the base plate's direction arrows pointing from your current position to your destination. Then rotate the faceplate until the colored end of the needle is inside the north-south arrow on the faceplate and the needle and north-south arrow are pointing in the same direction—in other words, the north-south arrow on the faceplate is pointing to magnetic north. Put the map away and hold the compass horizontally in your palm. As long as you keep the north-south arrow on the faceplate pointing to magnetic north and don't turn the faceplate, the base plate direction arrow will point you toward your destination.

This technique is also known as **taking a compass bearing**, because the direction arrow points at a degree measure on the faceplate. Thus, if you know your destination lies along a bearing of 30° from a certain point, to get there you rotate the faceplate until its 30° mark points in the same direction as the base plate direction arrow. Then, holding the compass horizontally in your palm, turn your body until the colored end of the compass needle sits inside the faceplate arrow—so that the needle and faceplate arrow are both pointing to magnetic north. Again, as long as you keep the north-south arrow on the faceplate pointing to magnetic north and don't turn the faceplate, the base plate direction arrow will point you toward your destination.

When you have to skirt a terrain obstacle such as a ravine, determine the compass bearing of the new direction of travel you're taking to get around the obstacle. As you hike in that direction, either count your steps or somehow estimate as accurately as possible how far you're walking off-course. Once around the obstacle, to get back on your original course you'll have to reverse the distance you traveled off-course at the opposite bearing. If your bearing heading off-course was 40°, then you'll have to follow a compass bearing at 220°—which is opposite 40° on the compass dial—until you've covered the same distance and returned to your original course. Then you'll turn back in your original direction of travel.

Buying a Map

Getting the right map is usually very easy: You walk into a store (or in some cases, a land management agency's office) and ask for a good hiking map covering the area, peak, park, or forest where you intend to hike. Besides traditional paper maps, you can now get maps from online sources and on CD-ROM. For popular destinations, such as national parks and forests, there are almost always commercial topo maps available for several dollars or less that provide all the information you need, including trails, contour lines, major land and water features (for example, summits, lakes), trailheads, and access roads. For hiking on trails, this is all you need.

If you're going to a more obscure destination, there may not exist a commercial topo map of that place, or if your hike demands a map that shows great detail (for instance, if you're hiking in an area without trails), many commercial topo maps will be inadequate. In either case, you'll need to purchase topographical quadrant maps, or **quads,** produced by the U.S. Geological Survey (USGS). The USGS has mapped the entire country on a grid, and its topo maps include information important to hikers, such as land and water features, topo lines, and trails. (Be aware that some quads were originally mapped decades ago and don't always show current trail locations. The year the map was made is printed below the map's name. It's a good idea to check with the land management agency about the accuracy of the map you're using.)

The standard size USGS quad used by hikers is the 7.5-minute quad, a term that simply refers to the amount of land the map covers. Longitude and latitude are measured in degrees, which are further subdivided into minutes (60 minutes per degree) and seconds (60 seconds per minute). A 7.5-minute quad shows a square 7.5 minutes of longitude and latitude, that is, a square patch of earth that's 7.5 minutes long on each of the four sides. (Remember, think of minutes and seconds as distance in this context, not time.) The 7.5-minute quads are on a 1:24,000 scale, meaning they show just half the area of a commercial topo map that's on a 1:48,000 scale, but because the map surface itself is usually of comparable size, the quads show much greater detail. For example, the contour interval is 40 feet, whereas it may be 100 feet or higher on a commercial topo map. All USGS quad maps have names appropriated from a major landmark that appears on the map, such as a peak. Stores that sell USGS quads also have a large key map that shows all of the quads (and their names) overlaid on a map of that state; by looking at the key map, you can determine which quads cover your destination.

See Appendix A for a listing of major mapmakers, including the USGS.

Trail Signs

Trail signs are placed at trail junctions and other key points on many trails, though you should not assume a trail will be signed. You'll find signs on many popular, well-maintained trail systems. They may provide only the names of the trails that meet at that junction or provide additional information like arrows indicating the direction to walk to reach key points, such as a trailhead, summit, or ranger station, and the distances to those points. Good signs are extremely helpful, but sometimes signs give incorrect distances—usually they're not off by too much, but an error of even 0.3 mile is significant when you're walking and trying to estimate how far you've gone. Signs may also be missing, perhaps damaged or knocked over in a storm and covered in brush. The point is to not presume that signs will guide you along a hike.

The other basic navigational aide available on many trails—and usually on popular trails—is a **trail marker,** or **blaze.** Trail markers may consist of the following:

- ▲ Paint slashes on trees or rocks
- ▲ Plain plastic or metal markers on trees along the trail
- ▲ Rough notches chopped in the bark of trees with a hatchet
- ▲ **Cairn,** or rock piles, that are obviously not naturally occurring (thus distinguishing them in a landscape that may be very rocky). Cairns are spaced at regular intervals above tree line, where there are no trees and where rocks may be covered with snow. Cairns are used because they are easier to spot from a distance than paint slashes on rocks when the entire ground is covered with rocks.

Blazes and plain plastic or metal markers will typically be in one consistent color for a trail, though the color may be different if you turn onto another trail. For example, the entire 2158-mile length of the Appalachian Trail (AT), from Springer Mountain in Georgia to Mount Katahdin in Maine, is marked with white blazes on trees and rocks (and cairns above tree line), while side trails connecting to the AT are typically blazed in blue. A hiking guidebook or map will often indicate the color of a trail's blazes.

Using All of Your Senses

Whether on the trail or the street, some of us also seem to have an innate ability to figure out which direction we need to go; others get easily confused. Why is that? Some researchers believe the answer lies deep within the brain, embodied by an actual "sense" of direction that can be trained. To improve your sense of direction, get out and test it from time to time. Here are some tips on improving your ability to figure out where you're going on the trail:

- ▲ Before your hike, study the maps to get the lay of the land, imagining what the valleys, streams, and mountains will look like in relation to one another, and store these images in your memory.
- ▲ Allow plenty of rest time before and during your trip. Studies show the brain is more adept at receiving and storing spatial relationships when well rested.
- ▲ Practice identifying north, south, east, and west in relation to your surroundings.
- ▲ Learn constellations, particularly the North Star, so you can locate true north no matter where you are. It won't necessarily help you hone an internal sense of direction, but it may help you keep your bearings.
- ▲ Resist the urge to charge down the path. Pause, and orient yourself by noting the general compass direction you'll be heading. Check to make sure it matches what you see on the map.
- ▲ Physically point back toward the trailhead once you reach a campsite. Research has shown that people are more likely to guess correctly and remember directions if they physically point in the correct direction. Practice "learning" directions by pointing and guessing, then confirming or correcting with a compass and map.
- ▲ Recite aloud the prominent landscape features that you pass on your travels, especially when you're off-trail or in an area where markings are few. For example: "Lake on the left, hill on the right, walking through aspen grove." Studies have shown that verbally expressing this information helps store it in your memory more effectively than simply reading and observing.
- ▲ Put on a blindfold in camp and have someone lead you in a random direction and accompany you as you try to find your way back unblindfolded. One researcher suggests this helps you use your other senses (particularly smell and hearing) to memorize the route.
- ▲ Stay focused on the terrain; don't let conversations or daydreaming distract you.
- ▲ Take a mental snapshot every 10 minutes as you hike. To find your way back, simply reverse the images.

The Good, the Bad, and the Ugly

When hiking in a place where the trails are easy to follow—that is, they're well maintained and clearly marked—finding your way is usually like a walk in the park. Popular trails are often maintained so that hikers can find their way easily along them. This is done deliberately by management agencies, such as state and national parks, both to prevent people getting lost and to avoid the damage to the landscape that can result from many hikers inadvertently wandering off-trail, trampling vegetation, and creating rogue paths that cause erosion. If you're looking for trails that are easy to follow, a good hiking guidebook or a helpful park employee at

Watch your footing on steep trails. Hikers here attempt the short but steep hike up The Beehive in Maine's Acadia National Park.

the visitor center information desk can point you in the right direction. Not only are you less likely to get lost on such a trail but the path is also often maintained well so that you're less likely to turn an ankle (though this is certainly not always true), the trail is often safer for children, and it is popular for its scenic value, meaning it's probably a beautiful hike.

Conversely, trails that are not well maintained, and not regularly marked with signs, blazes, colored markers, or cairns, can be enormously difficult to follow. Trails such as this present a challenge that experienced hikers may relish but novice hikers may dread or even experience trouble on. The trail's treadway, or actual footpath, may be narrow and obscured by brush or not at all visible because it receives little foot traffic. Footing might be very difficult on ankle-turning rocks. Rough trails such as this are often found in remote wilderness areas, but they may also be found on the same public lands as popular, easy-to-follow trails. Some long trails may be well marked in some places and difficult to follow in others. The Continental Divide Trail, for instance, is a good path in some places but rough and obscure in many others. If you're unfamiliar with the area, find out from the management agency beforehand how well the trails are signed and blazed.

Global Positioning System

"Whoa! I need a GPS receiver to go hiking?!" Did you just think that thought? The answer is unequivocally, "No." For many hikes on good trails, a good map and a compass for insurance are all you need. However, some people (and this could be you) want to explore remote terrain where navigating becomes very tricky because of faint or nonexistent trails and ubiquitous terrain—including places such as Alaska and parts of the West's mountain regions. For those folks, a **Global Positioning System (GPS)** receiver can come in very handy—and keep them from getting lost. Therefore, a simple explanation of how they work is in order.

A GPS receiver picks up navigational signals from government-operated satellites circling about 12,000 miles above the Earth's surface. Once a unit gets data from three of the twenty-four satellites, it determines your location and displays it on a liquid crystal display (LCD) screen in terms of latitude and longitude (or your choice of other coordinate systems)—so you still need a map and the know-how to figure out where exactly you are. If the receiver gets data from four satellites, it can provide altitude, too. When you preprogram the receiver with the coordinates of a specific location—called a **waypoint** in GPS-speak—and tell the unit to "go to" that location, you'll get an on-screen arrow pointing you in the correct direction. What most GPS receivers cannot do is tell you whether a terrain feature like a cliff or deep ravine is barring your path; you'll have to read your map to figure out how to get around such things. Some of the best GPS receivers allow you to download a topo map into them, but reading that map in detail on a tiny LCD screen is difficult.

A good GPS receiver works in most weather conditions and regardless of visibility. When night falls, simply turn on the screen's backlight. You can mark the spot where you entered the trail, and if you need to find your way back to civilization quickly, most GPS receivers have an instant "reverse route" feature to help you backtrack. (In fact, unless you store your starting point before you leave the trailhead, your GPS receiver cannot lead you back.) A GPS receiver will store, or remember, hundreds of waypoints and allow you to program and store dozens of routes, which consist of a series of waypoints. Most GPS units even give you an estimated time of arrival and a warning when you stray off course. This technology is evolving rapidly; expect much to change during the life of this edition of this book.

Many GPS receivers weigh less than a pound and fit easily inside a shirt or pants pocket, which is important if you're carrying it on a long walk. The best can be held and operated with one hand. GPS receivers drain batteries quickly, especially in the cold. Get one with a battery-saver feature that will shut the unit down in 5 or 10 minutes, and consider spending the extra money to get a long-life, rechargeable lithium battery, which also weighs less, lasts longer, and withstands cold better than an alkaline battery.

Many models now are **multichannel,** or **parallel-channel, receivers,** with twelve channels that can lock onto several satellites at once, providing a steady stream of information. Parallel-channel devices can get a fix on at least three satellites and calculate your position in less than 2 minutes. They're powerful enough to work in dense forests and deep valleys. GPS receivers vary greatly in the variety of features they offer and in how their modes of operation are organized. Some are more complex and take longer to learn to operate than others—which may also translate to greater versatility once you do learn it, though not always. If you're interested in getting one, try out different models in the store and see which you find most intuitive to use. A GPS receiver is a complex gadget, but you shouldn't have to be a NASA mission control specialist to operate it. Look at the receiver and read the instruction book. Even without peeking at the instructions, you should be able to get and store waypoints and plot out a simple Point A to Point B route.

GPS receivers can be great navigational aids in low-visibility conditions or other difficult circumstances. However, ultimately, they do not substitute for good map-and-compass skills. Learn to use your compass and read a map before trying to advance to something relatively more complex such as a GPS receiver.

"Temporarily Lost"

It always makes for a great headline when people lose their way on a hike and prompt a search: "Rescuers Find Lost Hikers Alive." In reality, of the tens of millions of Americans that go hiking every year, few actually get so "lost" that they spend an unplanned night outside and someone has to go looking for them. Even those who do get "lost" are often not far from the nearest road and fast-food restaurant or at least the nearest ranger station. With a little knowledge of how to find their way (another good reason to learn some basic map and compass skills), they might have avoided the uncomfortable night outside and all the media fanfare.

The odds are that, even if you turn into an avid hiker for life, you'll never be one of those people who make the headlines—especially if you plan and choose your hikes sensibly. More likely, you will occasionally have the experience of being **temporarily lost**. When on a trail you don't know intimately, it's often impossible to ascertain exactly where you are—and it usually doesn't matter any more than it matters whether you know exactly where you are on an interstate highway at any given moment. All that's really important is that you know where you started, when you're at key points along your route, and how to get where you're going.

What happens when you don't reach an expected juncture along your hike, or lose the trail, or suddenly realize you're not sure which way to go to reach your destination? Well, you're "temporarily lost." There's no need to panic. You're probably not far off course. Keep your head together and methodically try to figure out where you should be, and you'll get there without anyone having to call out the search party. Try the following techniques:

▲ **First, don't strike off bushwhacking off-trail aimlessly looking around in hopes of finding your way.** That's the best way to get really lost. Take a good look around and pick out a distinctive landmark such as a big tree or rock, so that you'll recognize this place again if necessary. That spot may become your **ground zero** for finding your way out of there, or you may somehow travel in a circle and wind up back there again.

▲ **Remember which direction you came from to reach this "temporarily lost" point.** Don't get turned around and completely disoriented, which is easy enough to do in an environment such as deep forest, open desert, or alpine terrain where everything looks the same (especially to someone who's getting a little nervous).

▲ **Confirm whether you are indeed off course.** While remaining where you are, gaze in every direction for signs of the trail—including behind you. You might see a marker that shows you're actually on the trail, though the path may be indistinct. Perhaps a tree may have blown down, obscuring the trail although it's right nearby. Carefully scout your immediate area; the trail may just be hidden from view.

▲ **Think about the last time you were certain you were on the trail and how long ago or how far back that was.** Knowing that, you can estimate the maximum distance you could have possibly wandered off course. Then look at your map and your surroundings to see whether you can identify land features that are within the distance you might have walked from your last known location. This might help you pinpoint, at least approximately, where you are; then use your map and compass to determine which direction to walk to find your trail or get to safety.

▲ **If you're certain you're off course, the first logical strategy is to backtrack until you rejoin your trail or reach a spot that's identifiable on the map or that you recognize and whose location you know.** Look for signs of the trail, such as packed soil and a worn footpath. At that point, you may be no longer temporarily lost. Don't rush, and keep track of the time (so you'll have some idea of how far you're walking), of where you're going, and how to get back to your ground zero, the place where you first realized you were temporarily lost. If while supposedly backtracking you've actually struck off in a wrong direction, you'll need to get back to that ground zero spot again to try another strategy.

▲ **If none of these strategies work, you strike off from your ground zero point in one direction at a time looking for a known location.** For instance, using your compass, first walk in a straight line due north from ground zero for 10, 20, or 30 minutes—whatever distance seems reasonable. If you find no sign of a trail or anything recognizable to you or identifiable on your map, return to ground zero and walk a similar length of time in a straight line due east. Do the same thing heading south and west, if necessary.

If You Are Lost

If you are absolutely, irreversibly, undeniably "lost"—that is, all of your efforts have not brought you anywhere you recognize or can identify on the map—you must remain calm because panicking only worsens your situation. You have two choices:

1. **Walk downhill or follow running water downhill (if you're in mountains).** This may eventually lead you to a road or human habitation. This is only a good strategy in a populous area; in a remote area with few roads and communities, this will likely only get you more lost.

2. **Return to your ground zero spot.** To the best of your knowledge, ground zero is closer to where you should be than anyplace else you've explored in trying to find your way out; wait there for help to arrive. If you are absolutely lost, this is the smartest strategy because searchers will designate their search area based on how far you could possibly have walked from your known starting point since you began your hike. The more you wander aimlessly, the more likely you are to wind up farther away from your hike's start; the closer you are to your hike's start, the sooner searchers are likely to find you. Move only if you can safely get to a spot where you're more visible, such as an open meadow.

To help searchers find you, provide clues. Break branches, tie ribbons, and build rock cairns in conspicuous locations. Light a fire (safely) to provide smoke signals by day and light by night. If you do have to move, leave notes. Use paper and pen, mud on rocks, or sticks in the dirt. Whistles have saved countless hours of search time; blow yours regularly in three short blasts. Use a mirror or other reflector to signal planes or distant searchers. If you spy a low-flying plane, lie flat on your back in an open area with your arms outspread. This makes you much easier to recognize from above than if you were standing vertically waving your arms.

In the meantime, maximize your comfort. Set up your tent or build a shelter out of whatever you can find if the weather requires it. Make sure that the shelter doesn't hide you from searchers on foot or in the air.

If you are lost but on a trail, stay on it—you're more likely to encounter other people on a trail than off-trail. And if you decide to try to find your way out rather than waiting for help, trails are much easier and faster than bushwhacking off-trail, and they will eventually lead to civilization.

Avoiding getting lost is really no more than a mental exercise. While hiking, don't let conversation or daydreaming distract you from keeping track of where you are and where you want to go. Watch constantly for trail markers, junctions, and obvious landmarks. If you're attentive, you'll never wander far off the trail before realizing your error, which makes correcting it much easier and faster. If circumstances result in rescuers looking for you, they'll find you much more quickly if you've left your hiking itinerary and the time you intend to finish with someone who'll know if you're late returning from your hike.

Crossing Water

Here's a news flash that will come as no surprise to you: **Fording,** or wading across moving water such as a river or stream, can be dangerous. However, what many people don't realize is that moving water can be more dangerous that it initially appears, including relatively shallow streams. Occasionally while hiking, you'll run into a stream or creek that isn't crossed by a bridge, and you'll have to decide on the safest spot to cross—or whether to cross at all. Remember the following tips:

▲ **Know before you go.** Before your hike, check your map and ask a ranger whether there are any stream crossings and how deep or difficult they may be, knowing that crossings are often more difficult in spring and early summer and may be impossible at some times of the year. If you anticipate getting your feet wet, especially if the water's cold, consider bringing extra socks or waterproof socks and hardy, strap-on sandals (not flip-flops).

▲ **First, don't attempt anything with which you're not comfortable.** Assume the crossing will be harder than it looks, especially where big rocks complicate the flow, and turn back if you're not sure it's absolutely safe. Slow-moving water less than waist-deep can often be waded safely, especially where you can see the bottom and it's sandy or the footing looks secure. Don't think only foaming white water is dangerous. Swift water that's up to your knees or deeper can be difficult to cross, and swift water that's more than waist-deep is often too dangerous to attempt. Small stones, smooth rocks, and algae-covered rocks on a stream bottom can be slippery.

When fording moving water, use two poles or sticks and change into sandals or old sneakers to keep your boots dry.

- ▲ **Consider alternatives to crossing a fast current.** Look around for a log bridge or a line of stones across the river, but be careful: Logs and stones that are wet or smooth can be treacherously slick. Check your map to see whether the trail soon crosses back over to your side again, in which case you might be able to just stay on that side and rejoin the trail. In addition, check whether there's a tributary stream feeding into the one you're thinking about crossing just up-stream from your spot. Crossing above a tributary might be easier because there's less water volume in the main current than below the tributary.
- ▲ **If possible, ford the waterway in the morning.** Creeks and rivers that originate in glaciers or snowfields are lowest in early morning and highest in late afternoon because daytime sun and warmth accelerate melt-off while the cold of night slows it down.
- ▲ **If you deem the stream safe enough to ford, find a spot where it's wide and shallow or braided in multiple channels.** Steer clear of big boulders, which can make a current unpredictable. Give a wide berth to any standing waves in the river; they indicate deep water and a submerged boulder.
- ▲ **Be aware of downstream hazards such as a waterfall or cascade, rocks, or a tree with branches that has toppled into the river.** If you are carried downstream, anything like that can be dangerous.

▲ **If the water's higher than your boot tops, take off your socks and boots and secure them to your pack or tie the laces together and drape the boots around your neck.** Change into sandals or old sneakers to protect your feet from rocks. Seal valuables such as a camera in watertight bags and put them inside your pack.

▲ **Use trekking poles or find a pair of stout walking sticks for balance.** Loosen your pack straps and unfasten your hipbelt and chest strap. You may have to be able to get the pack off quickly if you fall. While crossing, look straight ahead—staring down at moving water can make you dizzy and cause you to lose your balance. Don't worry—your brain will remember where to step. Probe ahead with your walking sticks, moving just one foot or stick at a time. Don't rush: Fording a swift current safely takes patience. If necessary, cross with your companion(s) and brace against one another, with the stronger person in front to take the brunt of the current.

▲ **If you do fall, don't panic.** Hopefully, you've chosen your crossing wisely and your only risk is getting wet and a little embarrassed. Carefully get back to your feet. Try to keep your pack from going under or being carried away, but don't risk hurting yourself to save it. Re-collect yourself and either continue across or turn back, depending on your assessment of the situation.

"It's D-d-d-dark Out!"

Whether deliberately or accidentally, sometimes we find ourselves hiking after dark. I've done it many times, under both circumstances. It can be enjoyable on a calm night, under a fat moon or millions of stars and the glowing streak of the Milky Way—as long as you play things a little more carefully. You may one day find yourself wanting to hike after dark—say, you're camping or on a hut trip, it's a gorgeous evening, and you want to take an hour-long walk under the night sky. If so, you'll be much less likely to get lost or to turn an ankle if you remember these pointers:

▲ Time your hike for a clear night under a full moon, which casts a surprising amount of light.

▲ Stick with a trail that's obvious and well-maintained, rather than a minefield of big rocks and slick roots.

▲ Make sure you or someone in your party is skilled at following difficult trails in daylight.

▲ Darkness magnifies distances in our minds and distorts our sense of time. Pay attention to the time, your walking pace, and your map to know how far you've gone and where you are.

▲ Move slowly, watching the trail as you step to avoid falling.

▲ Carry at least two reliable flashlights or headlamps and extra batteries, checking all the batteries before you head out.

Hiking at night is not as crazy as it may seem, as long as you have a good headlamp and carry extra batteries.

- ▲ Remember it's usually colder at night; dress appropriately, in layers (see Chapter 3).
- ▲ If you're in bear or mountain lion country, don't hike alone after dark.
- ▲ Make conservative decisions: Everything becomes more dangerous in the dark, from stream and creek crossings to negotiating your way through talus (which is a slope of large rocks and boulders) to evacuating an injured person.

If you find yourself unintentionally hiking after dark, much of the above advice still applies. Most of all, don't panic or assume that being out after dark means trouble. Recall what you learned in Chapter 3 about dressing to stay warm without overheating and what you've read in this chapter about finding your way and what to do if you're "temporarily lost." Keep eating and drinking to maintain your energy level and to help you stay warm. Think through your situation and calmly come up with a plan to get where you want to be.

Hiking in Winter

Why not hike in winter?! If you've developed many of the skills necessary to hike from spring through fall—and especially if you're confident hiking in the mountains during the warmer months, where you still need to know how to deal with cold, winterlike weather—then hiking from late fall through early spring requires nothing more than applying that same body of skills and knowledge to a situation that merely involves colder temperatures. I'm not talking about snow skills like snowshoeing or cross-country skiing or skills and equipment for walking on frozen, icy surfaces. Other books get into those activities in detail. I'm talking only about hiking on ground that's dry or perhaps wet but not frozen. There are many places in this country where you can hike trails in winter that are often free of snow and ice, from southern New England to many parts of the Southeast and Southwest, and much of the western seaboard.

You might ask, "Why go hiking in winter when you know it's going to be cold outside?" I would turn the question around to ask, "why not?" First, you go for all the same reasons that you hike in the warmer months: scenery, exercise, quietude, the chance to see nature and wildlife, and the wonderfully unfettered pleasure of walking in the woods and mountains. Those motivations don't disappear because the mercury shrinks. However, the outdoors does go through an amazing transformation in winter that's well worth seeing, and it varies depending on the climate and topography of where you hike. Trees become bare of leaves, opening up longer views in wooded areas. The air becomes drier, crisper, and clearer, which also means those longer views are unimpeded by summer haze. You don't have the bugs and heat. There are far fewer people on the trails. It's amazingly quiet. Go to the right place at the right time and you might see a wonder of nature not seen any other time of year, such as a frozen waterfall.

Winter hiking is often actually not such a cold experience, believe it or not. As you know from hiking at other times of the year, your body generates a lot of heat during exertion. Even in temperatures in the high teens or twenties, many people are comfortable hiking in a light fleece or shell jacket, or even in shirtsleeves—assuming it's a warm, long-sleeve shirt, there's no wind, and you're working hard. If you pick a hike that's protected from wind by dense forest, you might find the weather conditions surprisingly mild and unintimidating.

So give winter hiking a try—you might be surprised at how much you enjoy it. When you go, take note of these following tips:

- ▲ **Do some winter-specific research before choosing your destination.** Some places you hike in summer may be snowbound (which is fine if you're prepared for snow), exposed to frequent high winds, or may not be accessible or open in winter. The "beginner" hikes you did the first summer you took up this activity—say, in the local state park—might be a good place to introduce yourself to winter hiking.
- ▲ **Always check the weather forecast.** This allows you to avoid possible storms or even high winds, which in cold temperatures create an effect known as the **wind chill**, which lowers the effective air temperature and can be uncomfortable or even dangerous.
- ▲ **Eat and drink to stay warm.** Although you may not feel you're sweating much, winter's dry air dehydrates you quickly, and besides potentially causing muscle cramps and reducing your energy level, dehydration can reduce your body's ability to keep itself warm. Drink as much fluids as you would on a hot day. Eating plenty of food is also critical to staying warm in winter—another benefit of winter hiking. (See Chapter 4.)
- ▲ **Layer your clothing.** Layering with synthetic clothing (see Chapter 3) becomes even more important in winter. The objective in layering is to find a balance between your exertion level and how much clothing you're wearing that keeps you warm without causing you to perspire so heavily that your clothing gets wet, which will make you feel cold. Gloves or mittens and a hat or earband are standard fare in winter.
- ▲ **Bring extra clothing.** Always carry extra layers, in case the temperature drops abruptly or the wind kicks up. You will cool down quickly in the cold when you stop for a short rest, enter an area exposed to wind, or transition from walking uphill to a long downhill. Put on the extra clothing you'll need as soon as you stop or start going downhill, *before* you feel cold.
- ▲ **Bring safety gear.** Depending on where you're going and how long you'll be out, carrying some safety gear might be advisable, such as a sleeping bag and space blanket, just in case someone gets hurt and you have to keep that person warm until help arrives (which could take hours).

Keep Smiling

That bit of advice may seem gratuitous, but it's worth taking to heart. One of the most appealing aspects of hiking is the fact that we escape civilization. However, by escaping civilization, we lose control over our environment. Things don't always go as planned or hoped. Rain, hail, or snow can fall unexpectedly. The wind can be strong and cold. Your feet may get blistered or just hurt. You'll get tired.

The purpose of this book is to teach you how to avoid or deal with these and other mood darkeners, but there's no way to harness and manipulate nature completely (and let's hope there never is). The one thing you can control is your attitude. There's nothing worse than having to put up with a grumpy, complaining hiking partner. Research shows that positive-thinking people are better problem solvers, that optimism releases endorphins that create a natural high and mask pain, and that pessimism is tiring. Maintaining a sense of humor and a positive attitude is your best weapon against the unexpected. That, more effectively than any clothing, gear, or technique, will get you through the worst situations.

Watching Wildlife

Animals move quickly, are stealthy, and generally try to avoid getting close to humans. To watch them, you'll need (1) a strong telephoto lens, (2) a pair of binoculars (or spotting scope), (3) the knowledge of where animals hang out, and (4) the patience to remain still and quiet and wait for them. With most wildlife, the

Patient observers will see interesting wildlife, if you walk far enough away from civilization. These mountain goats are near Headquarters Creek Pass in Montana's Bob Marshall Wilderness.

best viewing times are in early morning and evening, when many animals are feeding and moving about (many species avoid moving in the hot daytime hours of summer). Field cards and books that help identify wildlife are helpful (see Appendix B). Ask a ranger for tips on good places to see wildlife—whether it's a big cliff to view raptors riding thermals while hunting or a lake to see moose feeding at dawn.

Wild animals are best when we leave them alone—don't try to get too close, and definitely do not feed wildlife. When you harass, scare, or chase an animal, you cause it to expend precious energy reserves eluding you, reserves it may need to get through the winter. Seeing wildlife in their native turf is exciting and one of the great rewards of hiking. Enjoy animals from a distance, for their sake and yours.

Outdoor Photography Tips

Photographs create a permanent memory of your hikes and give you a way to share the experience with other people. If you long to become an amateur shutterbug, read on.

Equipment

Choose a camera type based on your level of interest in learning photography. Point-and-shoot 35-mm cameras keep getting more sophisticated and versatile and offering better photographic quality. They are simple to use, lightweight, and small, but nonetheless they are more limited than true 35-mm single lens reflex (SLR) cameras. The latter will give you better photographs than a point-and-shoot, especially when shooting outdoor scenery, but SLRs have a much longer learning curve.

Subject Matter

Are you wondering what to shoot? That may become obvious the more time you spend outside, but the following are a few possible subjects:

- ▲ If you like plants, do a series of all the interesting ferns, wildflowers, shrubs, or trees (for example, leaves, bark, cones).
- ▲ If you like rocks, photograph all the interesting outcroppings or other formations.
- ▲ If it's people, think of the photographs as images for a storyboard. Start at the trailhead and be ready for each funny or significant moment.
- ▲ If you have a long lens and can adjust the shutter speed, get pictures of all the animals and birds you see.
- ▲ Trail signage, shelters, meals, the tent set up—all these add good documentary images to your hiking storyboard.
- ▲ Panoramas at high points are fun to look at when back home.
- ▲ To cover the technical questions, read the book *Photography Outdoors,* which is listed in Appendix B.

Photographs create a permanent memory.

Shooting Techniques

Think about these things when you shoot:

▲ **Compose** the photograph, which simply means to decide what to include in it. Composition is one aspect of photography where novices make errors that greatly affect the photograph's quality but where a little thought can greatly improve a picture.

▲ Compose the photograph to emphasize your subject, whether it's a person, the landscape, a person with the landscape as a backdrop, or the landscape with people in it for scale. Don't include anything that distracts from the subject or is uninteresting.

▲ Divide your image in thirds along its length (whether vertical or horizontal), and then place the elements of your image within those thirds. For example, instead of placing a person in the frame's center of a horizontal image, move her to the left or right side, and make use of a scenic background in the other two-thirds.

▲ When shooting a person, get close enough to have her fill or dominate the frame. Don't stand so far back that the subject appears small and distant.

▲ Capture the moment: Be ready to press the shutter at the right instant to catch a candid facial expression or as an animal lifts its head and looks directly at you.

▲ Shoot landscapes with a wide angle lens—between 17 mm and 28 mm—and place something in the near foreground, such as a big rock or stream, with mountains or other scenery in the background. This gives the photograph more depth and makes it more interesting.

▲ Don't shoot standing up beside your subject. Move around for an unusual perspective. Get on the ground, jump onto a boulder, or hike up a hill to overlook your subject.

▲ Watch the horizon through the viewfinder to make sure it's level—or conversely, to give a sense of fun or chaos, tilt the horizon in your photograph.

▲ Shoot when the sun is low—around dawn and sunset—when long shadows and strong contrast in the light give dimension and depth to a photograph. Shooting in the middle of the day, or under gray skies, usually produces flat, uninteresting photographs.

Remember, the more photographs you take, the better your chances of getting good ones—and of learning how to shoot better photographs next time around.

Chapter 7

When Nature Calls

We couldn't avoid this delicate subject any longer, could we? For many women who first take up hiking, one of their foremost concerns is the business of having to pee outside—never mind even the thought of doing No. 2 out there. This was certainly true for my mom, now in her sixties, when she first started hiking in her forties. It wasn't the threat of bears or getting lost, cold, or wet that made her anxious. On a day hike of several hours, she knew the time would come when she'd have to pay the piper and squat behind a tree or bush, and she did not look forward to that moment. She tried avoiding it, taking strategic advantage of the last available bathroom before we started any hike, holding out as long as she could on the trail, even deliberately minimizing her water intake until I convinced her of the folly in that. I'm happy to report that, while I'm sure my mother will never "go" outside unnecessarily, she does her business when she has to without too much complaint or dread.

The truth is that the thought of it is worse than the act—even the act of doing No. 2, which renders men and women equal in the eyes of Mother Nature. Most of us can comfortably avoid having to do that outdoors on day hikes of up to several hours, holding out until back in the comfortable realm of indoor plumbing, but if you hike enough, the day may come when you find your bowels unwilling to cooperate with your brain's desire to postpone their mission. When it does, it's important that you know exactly how to properly do this outside, where there is no flush to remove everything and other people are likely to stumble upon that same spot.

Use the Facilities, Please

One reality we can all celebrate is the surprising prevalence of outhouses in the backcountry and at trailheads. Actually, it's only surprising from the perspective of someone who's expecting a wilderness experience, though it's not a new or uncommon phenomenon in many popular hiking destinations. Land managers have installed and maintain these facilities along heavily used trails from the Appalachian Trail to California's John Muir Trail, otherwise the alternative would be thousands of people despoiling the environment and creating an unsightly health hazard.

You can easily find out from land management agencies or from some hiking guidebooks which trails have outhouses and where they're located, "relieving" you of any perceived unpleasantness associated with having to squat behind a tree. If there is an outhouse along your hike, use it—by doing your business there instead of in the woods, you help minimize the human impact on the place you're visiting. Ask the management agency whether they recommend that hikers use an outhouse for both urinating and defecating—in some places, agencies will ask hikers to only use the outhouse to defecate so as to slow the rate at which the outhouse pit fills. (If you'd prefer to pee in the outhouse instead of outside, of course, most land managers aren't going to object.) In other places, where the human traffic is heavy and the land is unable to "absorb" that much water waste, the managers might prefer hikers to urinate in the outhouses, also.

Outhouses and bathrooms are also frequently available at trailheads and at huts, shelters, and designated campsites in the backcountry, too. These will usually be marked on a map. Again, use them whenever possible for the sake of minimizing your impact on the environment. If you're at all squeamish about relieving yourself outdoors, you might want to seek out hikes on which you'll find such facilities.

The Moment of Truth

Okay, there are no outhouses or huts with bathrooms along your trail and to your mighty chagrin the two cups of coffee you gulped down while driving to the trailhead are moving matters along faster than you'd hoped. You're not going to make it back to the trailhead to seek some relief. You grudgingly accept that you're going to have to disappear into the woods for a while—and suddenly realize you're not sure how to do this.

Funny as it may seem, anyone who has never gone to the bathroom outdoors may find his or her introduction to the experience awkward and confusing. Most people living in industrialized societies are generations removed from having to

When above tree line, stay on the marked trail so as not to damage delicate alpine vegetation or create unofficial "trails" that exacerbate erosion.

squat outside, and we've lost that skill just as surely as most of us couldn't skin a buffalo or break a wild horse to save our lives. Years of sitting on a toilet bowl simply do not prepare you for doing it without a firm seat to rest your bottom.

Well, fear not. We're anatomically designed for squatting in the woods, and with a few tips on technique, we're all perfectly capable of this most basic of functions. After you've done it once or twice, you'll find it's actually quick and easy and not nearly as awful as you'd anticipated.

Before your hike, check with the land management agency where you're heading about any special policies or recommendations concerning human waste. Pack the following: a lightweight plastic hand trowel, toilet paper, doubled zipper-lock bags for packing out used toilet paper, and antimicrobial soap or towelettes for washing your hands afterward.

Yes, you did just read that you should pack out used toilet paper—always. Packing it out has become the recommended ethical practice in recent years. This practice replaces burying the paper (which would often be unearthed by animals or other natural forces, leaving nasty "white flags" strewn over the ground) and burning the paper (which never burns completely because it's not dry once used, plus burning is a forest-fire hazard in many mountain and desert climates). Stuff your used paper in doubled zipper-lock bags to reduce the chances of your foul cargo tearing open inside your pack, and store the bags in their own side pocket of your pack. Similarly, pack out all feminine hygiene products as well. To make this noble practice less noxious and more sanitary, saturate a small cellular sponge with ammonia and place it in the bag before you go. The ammonia will kill the offending bacteria.

The first step is to find a good spot. As obvious as this sounds, sometimes the inclination of someone who's feeling uncomfortable about having to do this at all will be to hurry up, take the first reasonable location, and get it over. Take your time. Feeling at ease doing it in the great outdoors, where there's no door to hide behind, takes some getting used to for the uninitiated. Take as much time as you need to find a spot that offers privacy, as much comfort as possible under the circumstances, and optimally, a sweeping view to inspire your moments of quiet contemplation. Don't pick a spot that's on too much of a slope or where you won't have good footing. Find ground that will be easy to dig into, like the loose soil often found at the base of a tree or below a large, dead log; your little pile will also decompose quickest in rich, dark soil that is somewhat moist and receives direct sunlight part of the day. Watch where you're stepping to make sure you're not rooting around in a place someone else has recently visited for the same reason. Be careful: You're going off-trail, which means footing may be more difficult and things such as branches can poke you in the eye and in various other places you'd rather not get poked.

Keep pristine waters pristine: Make sure you go to the bathroom at least 200 feet from any water source.

When you've selected your natural toilet, dig a **cat hole** for your deposit, using a trowel or a fairly flat rock with a sharp edge on it. (Make sure children and clueless adults understand that the trowel moves soil, not poop.) Leave No Trace (LNT) guidelines recommend that you go to the bathroom—whether urinating or defecating—at least 200 feet from water, trails, and other campsites (see the Introduction and Appendix A for more about LNT). The ideal cat hole is about 4 to 8 inches deep and 4 to 6 inches across, deep enough that animals won't dig up what you've left, yet shallow enough that solar heat will penetrate the soil and help decompose the waste. Be aware of this as you're looking for a spot, because often the soil in the mountains is thin with solid rock just beneath the surface.

Humans are designed to do their business from a squatting position, butt below the knees. Our lower intestine is engineered to evacuate most efficiently at this angle, which explains why anyone who has done the squat probably noticed that the whole process took less time and effort than sitting on a porcelain throne.

The primal squat, which is done freestanding without aid of a tree or rock for support, is no easy feat, though. Many of us simply don't use those muscles normally and find we can't hold that position for long. If necessary, look for support in nature to take the burden off your legs: Find a downed tree or rock to either lean back against or hold onto a downed tree, rock, or stout branch with your hands and arms extended in front of yourself as you lean back.

In the ideal primal squat, your feet remain flat on the ground and point slightly outward; thighs and calves brace against each other; and your butt is a few inches off the ground. Pull your pants just below the knees to allow freedom of movement with minimal risk of soiling clothes. As for aim, it'll land right behind your heels.

Once you're done, throw a handful of soil into the hole, along with any natural wiping materials used, such as leaves, and stir with a stick to speed decomposition. Use a trowel, rock, or stick to place at least 2 inches of topsoil over the hole. Before going on your way, camouflage the site with leaves and sticks.

Always, always wash your hands after doing your business. Human waste is bad stuff, and your hands will probably make contact with your face, mouth, water receptacle, and food (and possibly someone else's food) before your hike ends. Wash your hands with an antibacterial gel or towelette (available in drug stores and supermarkets), and deposit the towelette with your trash or used toilet paper.

Urine poses minimal health threats and is quickly absorbed into the soil. All the same, avoid peeing on vegetation because animals are attracted to the salts in urine and will defoliate any grass or shrubs you've watered. Sand or pine needles are fine places to relieve yourself.

Constipation is a common problem in the backcountry. One way to get things rolling in the morning is to drink cold liquid followed immediately by a hot drink— switching from cold to hot fluids triggers our gastric-colonic reflex. Eating dried and fresh fruit also helps. Equally unpleasant, especially in the backcountry, is diarrhea, which can be caused by too much heat and not enough fluids. Drink a lot, frequently. If you're worried about it, ask your local pharmacist for over-the-counter drugs to prevent diarrhea.

Nature provides us with many things that can substitute for toilet paper, relieving you of the burden of packing the paper in and back out (used). Substitutes include leaves that are still alive (not the dried ones on the ground); cones from spruce, fir, other conifer trees (avoid any with sharp points); sticks; and snow (wetter, denser snow works well; dry snow does not). Some hikers use natural materials exclusively, not bothering with toilet paper; others use them to do most of the work and clean up with a little toilet paper. You can bury natural materials with your feces.

For more on this subject, you may want to read the book *How to Shit in the Woods,* which is listed in Appendix B.

A Word for Women

Urinary tract infections are more common in women because of the anatomy of the female urethra. You might be tempted to not use toilet paper after urinating on a hike so that you don't have to pack out all the used toilet paper. Not only is this smelly and uncomfortable, it also increases the chance of a urinary tract infection, the symptoms of which are a burning sensation while urinating and increased frequency and urgency of urination. Use toilet paper when you urinate, especially if you are prone to urinary tract infections, and pack it out in doubled zipper-lock bags. On a day hike, used toilet paper won't take up much space, anyway.

Chapter 8

Weather

There's nothing like a beautiful, dry, sunny day while on the trail or enjoying the view from a mountaintop—and there's nothing in the laws of nature that guarantees you'll have such rosy weather every time you're out on a hike. When we go outside, we leave ourselves open to whatever Mother Nature wants to hurl our way, and the truth is we just don't always know what that will be. Weather forecasts aren't always reliable, especially for mountain regions where weather can be extremely localized and change quickly. It could be sunny and warm in the valley below as rain or snow falls on the mountain where you're hiking or raining in your valley and sunny in the next valley over.

In Chapter 3, you read about how to dress for any weather you might encounter on a hike. So now you're prepared for some amount of meteorological foul play—the question is how much of the wet and cold stuff you are ready and willing to tolerate. Then there's the matter of figuring out, while you're out on the trail, if and when it's time to revise your plans because of unexpected weather. In this chapter, you'll learn these four important skills:

1. What the important weather terms are, their basic concepts, and what these conditions look like in the sky
2. Where to get the most useable weather information for local areas before you leave home

Every hiker hopes for blue skies and dry air; desert hiking provides that, but conditions can change quickly, so carry clothing and equipment for the worst conditions.

3. How to do some weather forecasting of your own (sky and other factors) while out on the trail
4. How to decide when it's time to turn back or take emergency shelter

Weather Terminology

To understand weather forecasts, it's helpful to have a basic knowledge of some terminology. Here are some basic weather terms:

An **air mass** is a large body of air that's relatively uniform throughout in temperature and moisture level.

A **front** is the place where two different air masses meet, or collide.

A **cold front** is an atmospheric boundary where cold air is moving in to displace warm air.

A **warm front** is an atmospheric boundary where warm air is moving in to displace cold air.

Barometric pressure is a way of measuring air pressure. Barometric pressure below thirty is usually associated with stormy weather and with dry weather when above thirty. Rising pressure means the weather is improving; falling pressure means a storm is on the way.

High and **low temperatures** are typically provided in a forecast and refer to the warmest expected daytime temperature and coldest expected nighttime temperature. Although you may not be planning to spend the night outside, be aware of how cool it could be when you start hiking and how much and when it is expected to cool off so that you can dress appropriately.

Light rain and **thunderstorms**—for anyone who's never experienced the latter up close and personal—are very different. The former may slowly get you wet and cold if you're not properly dressed—but if you are properly dressed, you can easily hike in a light rain. Thunderstorms are violent and characterized by dangerous electrical activity in the atmosphere, high winds, and often heavy rain that can make it hard to simply see where you're going. Don't take thunderstorms lightly.

Wind is usually measured in miles per hour (mph) in the United States. On a day when the air is calm in valleys, there could be very strong winds on the nearby mountaintops, making it dangerous to hike above tree line because the wind could be strong enough to knock you over, or the wind speed combined with the ambient air temperature could create a wind chill effect that's cold enough to frostbite flesh. In approximate terms, most people would consider gusts of 30 to 40 mph strong, and winds of 50 to 60 mph make it difficult to walk. If you want a sense of how strong a 60 mph wind feels, stick your head out the window while driving that fast on the highway and ask yourself whether you want to be hiking in wind such as that.

Humidity is a measure of the moisture in the atmosphere, given as a percentage of what the air can hold. High humidity may foretell an afternoon thunderstorm, and at the least, it'll make you perspire heavily. Low humidity means the air is dry, and although you may not perspire heavily while hiking, your body will lose fluids quickly and you still need to drink plenty.

The **wind chill effect** refers to the combined effect of the ambient air temperature and the wind speed, given in degrees (Fahrenheit or Celsius), to represent the effective temperature. For instance, if the temperature is thirty-five degrees Fahrenheit and the wind is blowing 50 mph, it will feel like zero degrees to anyone in the wind. Knowing wind chill—especially above tree line, where you won't easily find protection from the wind—can help you decide how to dress or whether to postpone your hike for another day.

Checking the Forecast

As hikers, we're blessed to live in an age when information is widely and easily available and that includes information about the weather. For instance, from the time you get out of bed in the morning until you lock your car at the trailhead and start hiking, you might be able to find out that day's local weather forecast from any or all of the following possible sources:

▲ Television news or weather channels
▲ Commercial, public, or weather radio
▲ Daily newspaper
▲ World Wide Web (National Weather Service, *http://weather.noaa.gov/weather/ccus.html,* or other sites such as a commercial weather site or an area weather observatory)

- Land management agency where you're headed
- Posting at the trailhead or in a visitor center
- Posting or word-of-mouth in a local store or other business
- Other hikers in the parking lot

That list probably isn't even exhaustive in some areas. The point is, there's no reason to head out on a hike completely ignorant of the weather forecast. On the Internet, sources such as *www.weather.com* let you enter a ZIP code to get a localized forecast. You can get the local ZIP code for the area where you're hiking by asking a local person, checking your trail guide, going to a U.S. post office, or typing in the name of the nearest town on the U.S. Postal Service website *(www.usps.com)*. Localized forecasts for recreation areas can be found on the web and are often more accurate than forecasts given on nightly newscasts, which tend to be for the nearest urban area.

Sure, the forecast may prove inaccurate, but if the forecast calls for weather far nastier than you (or maybe anyone else) would want to get caught in, you'll feel awfully foolish finding that out after you've been soaked, shivering, or perhaps rescued from a mountain. Check the forecast, and consult more than one source if possible. The more local the forecast, the more likely it will be accurate for your purposes.

Pay attention to the forecast so you can hit the trail on days like this one at Alice Lake in Idaho's Sawtooth National Recreation Area.

Reading Between the Clouds

If you're on an easy, relatively short hike in a state park or someplace similar and can get back to your car within, say, an hour, then it matters little whether you can recognize different types of clouds and what they mean. You needn't be concerned with whether it's going to rain because you're not so far from the trailhead that it matters much.

However, when you're out on a hike of several hours and will at times be a significant distance from shelter—especially in mountains or anyplace where weather can change quickly and become severe—the ability to look at the sky and figure out what the weather is going to do can come in handy. It can help you decide on an appropriate course of action—whether to continue with the hike or retreat, or even find an alternate, safer route. Look to the heavens for some of the following simple but reliable cues:

White, puffy **cumulus clouds** don't always herald foul weather, but when they start to thicken, showers may be impending. If small cumulus clouds in the mountains become larger and resemble cauliflower, you can probably expect heavy rain or snow, gusty winds, and possibly thunder and lightning within an hour. The sharp edges of cauliflower cumulus softening at their outline indicate that ice crystals are forming, and thunder and lightning are likely to follow.

Wispy, high **cirrus clouds,** or **mare's tails,** usually arrive about 24 hours ahead of rain or snow.

A **lenticular cloud,** sometimes called a **cap cloud** because it looks like a giant bowl suspended upside-down over a peak, often forms above the highest mountain in the immediate area. They are a signal that stronger winds than you want to deal with are buffeting the summit and rain will probably arrive within 48 hours.

For centuries, mariners and others have known that a wide ring, or so-called **halo,** around the sun or moon is a reliable tip that rain or snow is likely within 24 to 48 hours; whereas, a **corona,** or close ring, around the sun or moon means rain or snow will start falling in 12 to 24 hours.

Learn the direction of **prevailing winds** where you're hiking. A land manager or hiking club member may know from what direction the wind usually comes. A change in wind direction usually signals a changing weather pattern, often for the worse.

If you're the type of hiker who likes gadgets such as altimeters—found in various models of high-tech watches these days—then you should know that your altimeter can act as a weather forecaster. An **altimeter** calculates your altitude based on the barometric pressure where you're standing. If your altimeter reading goes up when you have not changed altitude—for instance, if you notice a change in its reading when you haven't changed location—the barometric pressure has dropped, meaning a storm is approaching. If your altimeter drops when you have not changed altitude, the barometric pressure is rising and the weather is improving. An altimeter

Even on a sunny day, puffy cumulus clouds can transform quickly into a thunderstorm. Keep your eyes on the skies.

must be regularly calibrated to be accurate, though—that is, reset it to the correct altitude whenever you reach a known elevation such as a summit or a trailhead to ensure that subsequent readings are more accurate.

Thunder and Lightning

Few aspects of hiking in high places are scarier than finding yourself up there when a thunderstorm rolls in, lightning starts flashing, and thunder starts booming all around you. What may look like an impressive display of heavenly pyrotechnics from a safe haven in the valley can make your hair stand on end—for more reasons than one—when you're up high above the trees, in the midst of the flashing and booming, with no refuge in sight.

Of course, death or injury from lightning strikes is rare, even though many hikers and mountain climbers get caught too close to thunderstorms every year in this country. Most are lucky enough to escape unharmed, which tells you something about the likelihood of being struck even when you're in the wrong place at the wrong time. Still, you obviously don't want to get caught in the wrong place at the wrong time. If you plan to hike in the mountains, especially during the hot months of summer, which is the usual thunderstorm season, consider the following advice.

Afternoon summer thunderstorms are common in most mountains, especially where there is substantial barren terrain, which heats up under the sun faster than tree-covered terrain. As the land warms, it creates thermals of warm air that carry moisture upward, forming thunderheads. This upward movement of moisture is frequently helped along by winds hitting the mountains and being forced up the mountainsides, what is known as an **orographic effect.** Big lakes and oceans create thunderstorm conditions in the same way because water cools more slowly than land. Along many seashore areas, sea breezes start blowing inland by late morning as warmer air over land rises and cooler ocean air moves in. This creates a **front,** where thunderstorms develop. Just as thunderstorms in mountains are a threat to hikers caught in an exposed, high place, you want to avoid being near water, such as the ocean or a big lake, when a thunderstorm moves in.

The key is to get to safe ground before the thunderstorm hits. How do you recognize when a thunderstorm is forming? As a thunderstorm approaches, it may first look like a line of dark clouds on the horizon, or appear as clouds rapidly expanding upward and becoming taller than they are long, or take on the classic anvil shape of a thunderhead. You may start seeing distant lightning when the storm is within about 15 miles and hearing thunder once the storm is no more than 6 to 10 miles away. However, terrain and other noise may prevent you from seeing or hearing an approaching storm until it's just a few miles away. Another indicator of a nearing thunderstorm is a sudden gust of wind, which often comes up in advance of the front. Be careful not to mistake strong gusts created by terrain—common in a mountain pass or on a summit even on a bluebird day—for a thunderstorm wind.

It also helps to know the **flash-to-bang method** of calculating how long it'll take an approaching storm to reach you. Simply count the number of seconds between the flash of lightning and the crash of thunder. Five seconds equals a mile. A storm can advance 6 to 8 miles between lightning strikes, and lightning strikes have been documented 10 miles in front of a storm. In other words, don't assume you can ignore thunderclouds just because they're way off in the distance. If you can still count seconds between flash and crash, you have time to get to a safer spot. Do it, and then wait until 30 minutes after the storm passes to head out again.

What to Do If Lightning Threatens

▲ If at all possible, seek shelter in a building of decent size (as opposed to a tiny wooden shack) or metal-topped vehicle.

▲ Avoid isolated trees, metal (even in your pack's frame), and small shelters, because they attract lightning.

▲ Head for the rolling hills—that is, avoid stands of trees (long thought the best lightning cover) and instead seek gently rolling terrain. The reason: Strikes are random and unusual in low, rolling areas where there are few trees to attract lightning.

▲ If you're stuck among trees during a storm, avoid touching the trunks.

▲ Don't touch dissimilar objects, such as rock and ground or tree and ground.

▲ If your hair stands on end, metal objects or wet rocks hum, or you notice a bluish tinge of St. Elmo's fire (which is a shiny electrical discharge around objects) around boulders or a person, leave the area immediately.

▲ If you are caught without shelter in a thunderstorm, crouch in the **lightning position**—squatting with your feet close together—in a ravine or depression. Spread people in your group 15 to 30 feet apart so that not everyone is hit. Cover your ears to minimize hearing damage from thunder shock waves.

Lightning First Aid

If lightning strikes a fellow hiker, administer cardiopulmonary resuscitation (CPR) immediately. If he has a heartbeat but can't breathe, perform artificial respiration (tilt back his head, hold his nostrils closed, and breathe air into his mouth until you see his chest rise) for at least 30 minutes, the minimum time usually required before normal neurological function returns. Get the victim to a hospital as soon as he can breathe on his own.

Turn Back or Go On?

First of all, a little damp weather doesn't mean you have to turn and sprint for the car. In some parts of the country where rain or drizzle is a fact of life for months at a time, such as the Pacific Northwest, people would never get outside if they weren't willing to tolerate a certain level of wetness. Sometimes, especially in the mountains, what appears to be a big, ugly storm can turn out to be a passing shower. If precipitation begins while you're out on a hike and it would take you a while to get back to your car, anyway, then why automatically bail out on your plans if you face a hike in the rain either way? If you're prepared for wet weather, you don't necessarily have to bail out.

As strange or unpleasant as it may sound to some people, you can hike in weather that's not perfect—or simply make small changes to your plans in response to the weather, without completely canceling your hike. Assess the weather and where you are, and make a decision based on what feels sensible and comfortable to you. Are you high up a mountain above tree line? If so, a prudent decision would be to find the quickest route to get lower, into the trees, out of the storm's fiercest wind and away from areas most likely to be struck by lightning. Are you relatively protected from the rain and wind by forest and your clothing? If so, you can probably continue hiking, as long as you won't potentially put yourself at unreasonable exposure to the weather (for instance, climbing to an exposed summit) and the storm doesn't appear to be too severe. Is there any kind of shelter nearby, such as a backcountry hut, an overhanging rock, or even dense foliage, where you might take refuge for a while? You could hunker down and wait for the worst of the rain to pass, and then continue with your original plan. Look at your map and see what your options are.

Before your hike, check the forecast and prepare for the potential weather you could face. A rain jacket and perhaps a lightweight umbrella might get you through it all smiling. Pack all the clothing you anticipate possibly needing—and, depending on how far you're going, maybe extra warm clothing, just in case it's colder than you'd expected or some of your clothes get wet. As I already emphasized in Chapter 6, maintain a positive attitude and you'll get through most situations.

Better Safer Than Sorry: When to Turn Back

Of course, sometimes you should turn back or find the fastest route to civilization to escape weather that's really bad or for which you're simply not prepared. Consider ending your hike as soon as possible if you would answer "yes" to one or more of these questions:

1. Do you or any of your companions not have adequate clothing and boots for the weather and temperature? Not having the right clothing and footwear can result in hikers getting cold and wet and lead to injury or becoming stranded in the backcountry.
2. Is the weather so severe that visibility and your ability to find your way is compromised—or could become compromised farther along your route? Don't underestimate how bad things can get in the mountains. Beat a quick path out of there if there's any hint that the storm is more than a light rain.
3. Are you or any of your companions not comfortable with continuing the hike? Emotional discomfort with a situation may be your mind telling you that you're not ready for it, so it's often a good idea to follow your instincts.
4. Are you simply no longer enjoying yourself? Don't ever feel compelled to continue, either under pressure from someone else or because you're pressuring yourself to achieve some goal. Remember, this is supposed to be fun.

However, if you're prepared for wet weather, don't let a little shower spoil your fun. Get out there and enjoy it.

Chapter 9

Health and First Aid

I f you've been a diligent student and read everything in this book up to this final chapter, then chances are you may never have to apply any of the knowledge this chapter hopes to convey. Many backcountry accidents are the result of human error—of people underestimating the weather or other circumstances they face or of people overestimating their abilities or those of their companions. If you make conservative decisions on the trail, trust your instincts when they hint to you that something's not right, and avoid getting in way over your head, then you'll probably enjoy many years of pleasurable hiking without a single accident or injury. Hiking, after all, is certainly a relatively low-risk activity—there really is something to the old truism that the most dangerous part of any hike is usually the drive to the trailhead.

Then again, you never know. Accidents do happen, even to people who play it smart and make all the right decisions. (That's why they're called "accidents.") In addition, you might run into other hikers on the trail—people you don't know— who are in need of help. Not only is it a long-standing ethic among hikers to always help another hiker in need, I can tell you from experience that if you ever come across an injured person in the backcountry, regardless of your level of training in first aid or emergency medicine, you'll wish you knew even more about how to deal with medical emergencies. Therefore, at your leisure, read this chapter and consider it the beginning of your education in how to handle a backcountry medical emergency. As I'll reiterate later in this chapter, think about reading other books that specialize in this subject and taking a course. You might one day be happy that you did.

The objective of this chapter is to familiarize you with the most common ailments that might crop up on a hike—the sort of stuff you're most likely to encounter. This chapter doesn't cover the full gamut of things that can go wrong out there; that's better addressed in books and courses devoted to the subject of wilderness medicine, including some titles by The Mountaineers Books (see Appendix B).

First Aid

Ready-made first-aid kits are sold in many outdoor gear retailers and other stores, as are useful items such as pocket-sized first-aid manuals that cover the basics. These products are often all you need, although you should supplement such kits with any personal needs, such as prescription medications or a kit for handling a severe allergic reaction if someone in your party is allergic to bee stings or anything else to which they might be exposed on a hike—even a food allergy. If you have allergies or are carrying medications, tell your companions what and where those are and how to administer them in case you need help.

Of course, carrying a first-aid kit does you no good unless you know how to use it. Consider taking a course in basic first aid if you plan to hike regularly, especially if you hike in the mountains or on trails where you may be more than an hour from the nearest road or building. Courses are widely available from local Red Cross chapters, civic organizations such as the YMCA, and accredited wilderness first-aid instructional programs. Although any course can instruct you in the fundamentals of first aid, wilderness first-aid programs teach participants how to handle numerous types of medical emergencies and injuries in the backcountry, where advanced life support (that is, an ambulance and hospital) is not available within minutes of an incident. You may be on a trail within sight of the nearest road, yet evacuating an injured person could still take hours from your spot, because of the difficulty of moving someone in rough or wooded terrain. A wilderness first-aid course teaches you how to identify someone's injuries and care for that person during the hours that could elapse before the victim reaches a hospital. (See Appendix A for a listing of organizations providing wilderness first-aid instruction.)

First-Aid Kits

If you're preparing your own first-aid kit, besides personal items, pack the following basics in a sturdy zipper-lock plastic bag:

- ▲ Two large cravats
- ▲ Two large gauze pads

- ▲ Four 4-inch-by-4-inch gauze pads
- ▲ Several 1-inch adhesive bandages (for example, Band-Aids)
- ▲ One roll of 1-inch athletic tape
- ▲ A few safety pins
- ▲ One 6 inch elastic athletic bandage (for example, Ace)
- ▲ Several alcohol wipes
- ▲ A tube of povidone-iodine ointment (for wound care)
- ▲ Moleskin (for blisters)
- ▲ A knife or scissors
- ▲ A paper and pencil

Advice for Women

Don't let menstruation keep you from heading out on the trail. Bring ibuprofen for menstrual cramps. Because you should pack out sanitary products, tampons are a better choice than sanitary pads. Some female hikers prefer tampons without applicators because they are small and require less extraneous packaging to carry. After use, wrap the tampon in a piece of toilet paper and place it in doubled waterproof plastic bags in your pack, as with used toilet paper. Of course, you should never bury tampons—they take a long time to decompose, and animals dig them up.

Pregnancy doesn't have to keep you off the trails. Carrying a heavy pack is a bad idea during pregnancy because of the pressure the belt places on the baby and uterus. However, day hiking with a small pack that doesn't have a thick belt is fine. Better yet, let your partner carry the pack!

Don't exert yourself harder during pregnancy than you did before becoming pregnant. The exception to this rule is if you were a couch potato before becoming pregnant. Start a gentle walking routine or hiking on flat trails, gradually increasing your distances. Don't work so hard that you can't maintain a conversation. Avoid hiking in hot weather. Be extra careful about staying close to your doctor in the first trimester, when the risk of miscarriage is high, and in the third trimester, when the delivery date is near. Certainly, get your doctor's advice about hiking or any other physical activity during pregnancy.

Things That'll Get Ya

I hope that heading grabbed your attention. The ailments listed in this section really are the things that'll get ya while hiking—if you don't heed the advice offered in the preceding chapters. As you read on, you'll realize that the opposite is also true: that many of the problems detailed below can be avoided if you pay attention to the stuff covered in this book. Besides describing each ailment below, I'll tell you how to avoid and treat each one.

Blisters

Consider your average ripe peach. Press your thumb against the juicy fruit and gently move it back and forth. What happens? The skin moves under your thumb. Now press harder and rub. The skin rips and wrinkles, and peach juice dribbles down your hand. The same pressure-and-friction principle comes into play when you hike. The outer layers of your foot's skin can move more than the sensitive inner layers can. Boots and socks apply pressure and friction as you walk, causing these skin layers to separate and fluid to fill the void—a **blister.**

Now, let's get back to that peach. Say you dunk it in hot water. When you rub it, it peels more easily, right? Again, it's the same with your feet: Warm, moist skin blisters quicker than cool, dry skin. The obvious lesson here is to keep your peaches out of hot water. For starters, make sure your boots fit properly (see Chapter 2). Keep your feet dry, cool, and friction-free so you avoid blisters. Try supportive insoles, whether custom-made or over-the-counter—both types reduce movement inside a boot, thus limiting friction. Tend to hot spots the minute they develop on the trail. If you have a hot spot but no blister has formed yet, try putting a piece of athletic tape over it to prevent it worsening; you might finish your hike without ever developing a blister. Keep feet cool and dry; bring an extra pair of socks to change into if your feet perspire a lot or you expect them to get wet during the hike. In addition, if your feet tend to perspire a lot, bring talcum powder and use it to dry out feet and boots during rest periods.

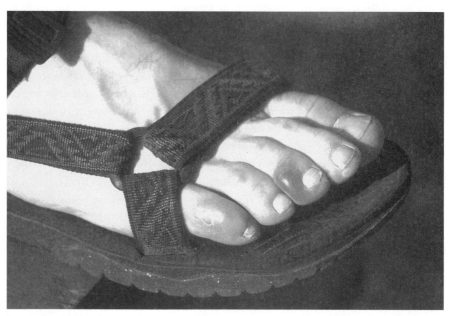

Poorly fitted hiking boots can create friction that eventually causes blisters, which this hiker suffers in Wyoming's Grand Teton National Park.

If you feel a hot spot developing on your foot, put a piece of athletic tape over it before a blister forms.

If you develop a blister on the trail, unless you're near your car or for any other reason you don't expect to walk much farther, pop and drain the blister before you continue hiking. To avoid infection, follow this procedure:

1. Clean the area with soap and water, alcohol, or an antiseptic towelette. Dry thoroughly.
2. Sterilize a needle or sharp blade, either by holding it over a flame (such as a match or butane lighter) until it's red-hot or submerging it in boiling water for 2 minutes.
3. Puncture the bottom end of the blister so gravity can help drain it. The opening should be no bigger than is necessary to remove the fluid. Starting at the top of the blister, massage the fluid toward the opening.
4. Apply antibiotic ointment to prevent infection, then wrap with the dressing or blister product of your choice. Blister-dressing products include **moleskin,** which is a soft fabric that adheres to the skin to protect the foot from rubbing against a shoe. Moleskin is widely available in drug stores and outdoor gear retailers. Standard plastic adhesive bandages don't hold well on your foot because of the friction and sweat caused by your shoe.

The following is the proper way to dress with moleskin or similar product:

1. Apply antiseptic cream directly to the blister and a layer of tincture of benzoin around the wound to help the dressing adhere.

2. Cut a circular piece of moleskin, molefoam, or your covering of choice that is a half-inch bigger than the blister. Cut a hole slightly larger than the blister in the middle of the covering and place the "doughnut" over the blister to create a pressure-free pocket around the sore.
3. Cover the entire doughnut with a second piece of moleskin, then secure it with duct tape. Run tape strips along the sides of your foot toward your toes, then secure the ends with a few loops around the instep.

Dehydration

It's just plain hard to stay hydrated when your body's working hard, especially on a hot day. You may often find yourself finishing a hike with a good thirst that demands quenching—that's no emergency. But **dehydration** does reduce your body's ability to do the many things it does, and you'll feel it while hiking if you get more than a little dehydrated: less energy, possibly muscle stiffness or cramps, or maybe a headache (especially if you're at 6000 feet or higher and genetically susceptible to altitude sickness symptoms). Severe dehydration can actually compromise your ability to make rational decisions.

Chapter 4 discussed the need to stay hydrated and how much to drink, and it pointed out that by the time you feel thirsty, you're already dehydrated and will be playing catch-up with your fluid consumption. The best way to know you're drinking enough is that you have to urinate regularly, and your urine is clear. The darker yellow your urine, the more advanced your level of dehydration; brown urine is a sign of severe dehydration, requiring emergency medical treatment.

Treating dehydration is as simple as avoiding it: Drink fluids, preferably water or an electrolyte-replacement drink (these come in powdered form that mix with water, so you don't have to buy the bottled versions). Drink steadily for a sustained period—it can take hours to bounce back from a level of dehydration in which you could finish your hike without problem, but your symptoms included a raging thirst and not having urinated for hours.

Sunburn

We all know about this one, but there are some common misperceptions about ultraviolet (UV) rays from the sun, which cause **sunburn.** There are somewhat heightened risks for hikers simply because they're exposed to the sun for hours at a time, and they walk to higher elevations, where there's less atmosphere to mitigate the effects of UV rays. The higher you go, the less atmospheric filtering of UV rays, thus the faster you'll burn. If you're hiking on snow—as you might do in a national park or forest in the Rockies, California's Sierra Nevada, or the mountains of the Pacific Northwest—be aware that snow reflects almost all of the sunlight hitting it, meaning you get UV light coming at you from all directions (which can cause nasty burns in weird places such as your ears). You know what sunburn looks like:

red, dry, peeling, maybe blistered skin that's sensitive. Don't buy into the old wives' tales that a tan protects your skin—it doesn't protect from UV exposure. Too much UV exposure can cause melanoma, an increasingly prevalent form of cancer in this country, and children's sensitive skin is particularly vulnerable (see Chapter 5 for more about children and UV exposure). Use a sunblock that has the highest skin protection factor (SPF) rating you can find that protects against UV A and B rays and is waterproof. Wear full-coverage sunglasses (your eyes can also be damaged by too much sunlight); a hat that shades your ears, face, and neck; and clothing that covers your skin as much as comfortably possible, especially if you have sensitive skin. To treat a burn, apply a moisturizing lotion and drink a lot of fluids.

Heat Exhaustion

Heat exhaustion commonly occurs in people who exert themselves outside without protecting themselves from the sun or heat with the proper clothing and by not staying well hydrated. It can even happen if someone is simply not used to the intensity of the heat or sun. Heat exhaustion is the result of the body losing salt and water through perspiration. Avoid this unpleasant feeling by drinking plenty of fluids, wearing a good sun hat, and using sunblock or clothing that provides good coverage—and simply paying attention to how you or your companions are doing if you or they begin to show signs of wilting from the heat. Symptoms of heat exhaustion include pale, cool, clammy skin, dizziness, nausea, slightly increased pulse and respiration rates, and sometimes vomiting and heightened anxiety or confusion. Usually someone suffering these symptoms bounces back after resting in a cool, shady spot for a while and drinking fluids for an hour (more or less); also, elevate the victim's feet while he or she rests. If symptoms persist more than a day, see a doctor.

Heat Stroke

Heat stroke is far more rare and serious than heat exhaustion, potentially leading to a coma and death without immediate care. Avoid this in the same way you avoid heat exhaustion, but watch closely for signs of heat exhaustion worsening. Among the symptoms of heat stroke are red, hot skin that could be dry or wet and a diminished level of consciousness that appears as confusion, disorientation, extreme agitation, or hallucinations. Remove the victim immediately from the heat and sun, cool the person by immersing him or her in water and fanning, and massage the limbs vigorously. Get the victim to a hospital right away.

Hypothermia

You've probably heard this term. The definition of **hypothermia** is simply a drop in the core body temperature caused by the body losing heat faster than it produces heat. It can happen in temperatures well above freezing. We've all known the feeling, especially as a child, from emerging from a swimming pool or lake and shivering from being wet—that was your body trying to rewarm itself from a mild bout with hypothermia, and it was easily remedied with a dry towel and a warm hug. When hiking, hypothermia can become a more serious threat if you're unable to escape a cold rain or wind quickly and are not dressed for it. You'll recognize it initially as a cold or numb feeling in your fingers, toes, hands, or feet. If allowed to progress, it can cause diminished physical coordination and alertness, confusion, apathy, disorientation, and shivering—in other words, someone suffering from hypothermia might not recognize the problem, so you have to watch your hiking partners for symptoms. In its severe form, hypothermia is characterized by slurred speech, convulsive shivering (which eventually ceases when the body can no longer produce the energy to shiver), then the apparent absence of a pulse or breathing and blue skin.

You know from previous chapters how to avoid hypothermia: Drink and eat enough food and fluids and dress properly for the weather (avoiding cotton). Pay attention and react to feeling your toes or fingers (or a companion's) if they stay numb or cold for more than 10 or 15 minutes. Someone suffering mild hypothermia (cold extremities, perhaps shivering) can be treated quickly on the trail by consuming fluids (a hot drink doesn't warm you faster, but it feels good) and food, adding more clothing (or changing from wet to dry clothing), and then moving to generate heat. A victim of severe hypothermia who can no longer produce body heat to warm up (and won't likely be coherent or able to walk) needs to be stabilized. Gently remove any damp clothing, change the victim into dry clothes, and then get medical help as quickly as possible. If you go on a hike anywhere that cold, wet weather is a possibility, bring a lightweight space blanket and extra clothes including gloves and a warm hat.

Soft-Tissue Injuries

Cuts, scrapes, bruises, lacerations, and punctures are classified as **soft-tissue injuries.** These occasionally happen to hikers, often because of a slip or fall, and are usually minor. Being careful is the best method of avoidance, but there's no foolproof method, and this stuff happens to kids on the trail. If someone falls, check the person out for any bleeding, which may not be immediately noticeable if covered by clothing. If there's bleeding, immediately apply direct, flat pressure to the spot—that will virtually always stop the bleeding if you're persistent. Anyplace where pressure could dangerously impede circulation, such as in the neck, try pinching off the wound instead. To reduce swelling, treat a bruise or swelling immediately with **RICE**—the acronym stands for **r**est (even if for 15 minutes), **i**ce (chemical ice pack, snow, immersing the swollen area in a cold stream, or even wrapping the injured body part in a wet shirt), **c**ompression, and **e**levation above the heart. Clean an open wound by flushing it with sterile water (the tap water or bottled water you're carrying should be fine), then bandaging it. Knowing how to wrap a sprained ankle or sprained knee and how to splint a damaged joint are two valuable skills one gets from a first-aid course.

Sprains and Strains

These are the last of the most common hiking injuries. **Sprains** result from over-stretching or tearing ligaments that support the bones around a joint, such as the ankle. **Strains** are tears in muscle tissue. Both are painful. Trekking poles or walking sticks enhance balance and help prevent the slips and falls that can cause these injuries. Sprains are immediately obvious because they're painful and cause immediate swelling; apply RICE (see previous paragraph) as quickly as possible, especially the ice. Muscle strains might feel like a burning sensation right away or not become painful until later (as with back strains). Some experts advocate applying ice to a strain immediately, followed in 24 hours by heat; some say use ice exclusively throughout the treatment of a strain. An antiinflammatory such as ibuprofen helps, too.

Other Health and First-Aid References

If you want to learn more about first aid in a backcountry setting, see Appendix B for suggested titles.

Appendix A:
DAY-HIKING RESOURCES

Mapmakers
DeLorme, 800-561-5105; *www.DeLorme.com.*
Earthwalk Press, 800-828-6277.
Green Trails Maps, 206-546-6277; *www.greentrailsmaps.com*
Topo!, 415-558-8700; *http://maps.nationalgeographic.com/topo/.* National Geographic topographic maps.
Trails Illustrated, 800-962-1643; *http://maps.nationalgeographic.com/trails/maps.cfm.*
USGS Map Sales, Federal Center, Box 25286, Denver, CO 80225. See the USGS website, *http://mcmcweb.er.usgs.gov/topomaps,* for a listing of businesses that sell USGS quad maps.

Conservation Organizations and Hiking Clubs
Adirondack Mountain Club (ADK), 814 Goggins Road, Lake George, NY 12845; 518-668-4447 or 800-395-8080, FAX 518-668-3746; *www.adk.org.*
American Hiking Society, 1422 Fenwick Lane, Silver Spring, MD 20910; 301-565-6704, FAX 301-565-6714; *www.americanhiking.org.*
American Rivers, 1025 Vermont Avenue NW, Suite 720, Washington, DC 20005; 202-347-7550; *www.americanrivers.org.*
Appalachian Mountain Club (AMC), 5 Joy Street, Boston, MA 02108; 617-523-0636; *www.outdoors.org.* The AMC has local chapters throughout the Northeast.
Colorado Mountain Club, 710 Tenth Street, No. 200, Golden, CO 80401; 303-279-3080, FAX 303-279-9690; *www.cmc.org.*
Green Mountain Club Inc., 4711 Waterbury-Stowe Road, Waterbury Center, VT 05677; 802-244-7037; *www.greenmountainclub.org.*
Idaho Conservation League, P.O. Box 844, Boise, ID 83701, or 710 N 6th Street, Boise, ID 83702; 208-345-6933; *www.wildIDAHO.org.*

The Grand Canyon from the roadside on the South Rim

Leave No Trace, P.O. Box 997, Boulder, CO 80306; 303-442-8222, FAX 303-442-8217; *www.lnt.org.*

National Parks and Conservation Association, 1300 19th Street NW, Washington, DC 20036; 800-628-7275; *www.npca.org.*

The Nature Conservancy (TNC), 4245 N Fairfax Drive, Suite 100, Arlington, VA 22203-1606; 703-841-5300; *http://nature.org.*

The Sierra Club, 85 2nd Street, 2nd Floor, San Francisco, CA 94105-3441; 415-977-5500; *www.sierraclub.org.*

Southern Utah Wilderness Alliance (SUWA), 1471 South 1100 East, Salt Lake City, UT 84105; 801-486-3161, FAX 801-486-4233; *www.suwa.org.*

The Wilderness Society, 900 17th Street NW, Washington, DC 20006-2596; 800-THE-WILD; *www.wilderness.org.*

Organizations Providing Backcountry-Skill Instruction (Including Hiking and Wilderness First Aid)

Stonehearth Open Learning Opportunities (SOLO), P.O. Box 3150, Tasker Hill, Conway, NH 03818; 888-SOLO-MED or 603-447-6711; *www.stonehearth.com.*

Wilderness Medical Associates, RFD 2, Box 890, Bryant Pond, ME 04219; 888-945-3633 or 207-665-2707; *www.wildmed.com.*

Wilderness Medicine Institute of National Outdoor Leadership School (NOLS), 284 Lincoln Street, Lander, WY 82520-2848; 307-332-5300, FAX 207-332-1220; *www.nols.edu.*

Peak-Bagging Lists, Organizations, and Clubs

Members of the **Adirondack Forty-Sixers Inc.** have climbed to the summits of the forty-six major peaks of New York's Adirondack Mountains. Adirondack Forty-Sixers, P.O. Box 9046, Schenectady, NY 12309-0046; *www.adk46r.org.*

Catskill 3500 Club members have climbed all thirty-five peaks of more than 3500 feet in New York's Catskill Mountains as well four designated peaks a second time in the winter. About half of the peaks are trailless and require bushwhacking and map-and-compass skills. The Catskill 3500 Club, 41 Morley Drive, Wyckoff, NJ 07481; *http://members.aol.com/howiedash/catskill_3500_club.htm.*

The Colorado 14ers is a list of fifty-four peaks higher than 14,000 feet in that state. Information about climbing these peaks can be found at the websites *www.14ers.com* or *www.colorado14er.com* and in Gerry Roach's guidebook *Colorado's Fourteeners: From Hikes to Climbs* (Fulcrum Publishing, 1999).

The Four Thousand Footer Club recognizes hikers who have hiked to the summits of all forty-eight peaks in New Hampshire's White Mountains that exceed 4000 feet in elevation. Four Thousand Footer Committee, 42 Eastman Street, Concord, NH 03301; *http://outdoors.org/activities/hiking/hiking-4kfooter-club.shtml.*

The Great Smoky Mountains 900 Miler Club is for hikers who have hiked all of the approximately 900 miles of maintained trails in Great Smoky Mountains National Park. For information, see the website *http://members.aol.com/gs900miler/*.

The Highpointers Club recognizes hikers who have reached the summit of the highest point in all fifty states. For information, contact R. Craig Noland, State Highpointers Club, PO Box 6364, Sevierville, TN 37864-6364; *cnoland@high pointers.org; www.highpointers.org*.

The New England Hundred Highest list consists of the 100 highest official summits in New England (including the New Hampshire Four Thousand Footers and Adirondack Forty-Sixers); the **Northeast 111** includes all "official" 4000-foot peaks in the Northeast: the traditional forty-six Adirondack peaks, the sixty-three New England 4000-footers, and two in the Catskills. Information about the New England Hundred Highest and the Northeast 111, plus other regional lists, is available at the website *http://home.earthlink.net/~ellozy*.

The South Beyond 6000 list consists of forty peaks in the Southern Appalachians higher than 6000 feet. For information, see the website *http://tehcc.org/beyo6000.htm*. You may also contact any of these clubs: Tennessee Eastman Hiking and Canoeing Club, c/o South Beyond 6000 Committee, P.O. Box 511, Kingsport, TN 37662; Carolina Mountain Club, c/o South Beyond 6000 Committee, Box 68, Asheville, NC 28801; Smoky Mountain Hiking Club, c/o South Beyond 6000 Committee, P.O. Box 1454, Knoxville, TN 37901.

Appendix B:
RECOMMENDED READING

Chapter 1: Getting Started

Berger, Karen. *Everyday Wisdom: 1001 Expert Tips for Hikers.* Seattle: The
Mountaineers Books/*Backpacker* magazine, 1997.

———. *More Everyday Wisdom:* Seattle: The Mountaineers Books/*Backpacker*
magazine, 2002.

Fenton, Mark. *The Complete Guide to Walking for Health, Weight Loss, and Fitness.*
Guilford, Conn.: The Lyons Press, 2001.

Musnick, David, and Mark Pierce. *Conditioning for Outdoor Fitness: A Comprehensive
Training Guide.* Seattle: The Mountaineers Books, 1999.

Ross, Cindy, and Todd Gladfelter. *A Hiker's Companion: 12,000 Miles of Trail-Tested
Wisdom.* Seattle: The Mountaineers Books, 1993.

Schad, Jerry, and David Moser, eds. *Wilderness Basics: The Complete Handbook
for Hikers and Backpackers.* 2d ed. Seattle: The Mountaineers Books, 1992.

Chapter 2: Gear

Lindgren, Louise. *Sew and Repair Your Outdoor Gear.* Seattle: The Mountaineers
Books, 1989.

Chapter 3: Clothing

Weiss, Hal. *Secrets of Warmth: For Comfort or Survival.* Seattle: The Mountaineers
Books, 1998.

Chapter 4: Water and Food

Miller, Dorcas. *Backcountry Cooking: From Pack to Plate in 10 Minutes.* Seattle:
The Mountaineers Books/*Backpacker* magazine, 1998.

Prater, Yvonne, and Ruth Dyar Mendenhall. *Gorp, Glop, and Glue Stew: Favorite
Foods from 165 Outdoor Experts.* Seattle: The Mountaineers Books, 1981.

Chapter 5: Children on the Trail

Evans, Lisa Gollins. *An Outdoor Family Guide to Lake Tahoe.* 2d ed. Seattle: The Mountaineers Books, 2001.

Ross, Cindy, and Todd Gladfelter. *Kids in the Wild: A Family Guide to Outdoor Recreation.* Seattle: The Mountaineers Books, 1995.

Chapter 6: Safety, Fun, and Trail Ethics

Burns, Bob, and Mike Burns. *Wilderness Navigation: Finding Your Way Using Map, Compass, Altimeter, and GPS.* Seattle: The Mountaineers Books, 1999.

Fleming, June. *Staying Found: The Complete Map and Compass Handbook.* 3d ed. Seattle: The Mountaineers Books, 2001.

Gardner, Mark, and Art Wolfe. *Photography Outdoors: A Field Guide for Travel and Adventure Photographers.* 2d ed. Seattle: The Mountaineers Books, 2003.

Graydon, Don, and Kurt Hanson, eds. *Mountaineering: The Freedom of the Hills.* Seattle: The Mountaineers Books, 1997.

Letham, Lawrence. *GPS Made Easy: Using Global Positioning Systems in the Outdoors.* 3d ed. Seattle: The Mountaineers Books, 2001.

McGivney, Annette. *Leave No Trace: A Guide to the New Wilderness Etiquette.* Seattle: The Mountaineers Books/*Backpacker* magazine, 1998.

Smith, David. *Backcountry Bear Basics: The Definitive Guide to Avoiding Unpleasant Encounters.* Seattle: The Mountaineers Books, 1997.

Chapter 7: When Nature Calls

Tilton, Buck, and Rick Bennett. *Don't Get Sick! The Hidden Dangers of Camping and Hiking.* Seattle: The Mountaineers Books, 2001.

Meyer, Kathleen. *How to Shit in the Woods.* 2d ed. San Francisco: Ten Speed Press, 1994.

Chapter 8: Weather

Renner, Jeff. *Lightning Strikes.* Seattle: The Mountaineers Books, 2001.

———. *Northwest Mountain Weather: Understanding and Forecasting for the Backcountry User.* Seattle: The Mountaineers Books, 1992.

———. *Renner's Guide to Mountain Weather.* Seattle: The Mountaineers Books, 1999.

Chapter 9: Health and First Aid

Steele, Peter. *Backcountry Medical Guide.* 2d ed. Seattle: The Mountaineers Books, 1999.

Tilton, Buck, and Frank Hubbell. *Medicine for the Backcountry: A Practical Guide to Wilderness First Aid.* Guilford, Conn.: The Globe Pequot Press, 1999.

Van Tilburg, Christopher. *Emergency Survival: A Pocket Guide.* Seattle: The
    Mountaineers Books, 2001.

————. *First Aid: A Pocket Guide.* 4th ed. Seattle: The Mountaineers Books, 2001.

Weiss, Eric. *Wilderness 911: A Step-by-Step Guide for Medical Emergencies and
    Improvised Care in the Backcountry.* Seattle: The Mountaineers Books/*Backpacker*
    magazine, 1998.

Wilkerson, James A, ed. *Hypothermia, Frostbite, and Other Cold Injuries: Prevention,
    Recognition, Prehospital Treatment.* Seattle: The Mountaineers Books, 1986.

Wilkerson, James A, ed. *Medicine for Mountaineering and Other Wilderness Activities.*
    5th ed. Seattle: The Mountaineers Books, 2001.

Index

About the Author

Freelance writer and photographer Michael Lanza is a contributing editor to *Backpacker* magazine and writes a monthly column and other articles for *AMC Outdoors* magazine; his work has also appeared in *National Geographic Adventure, Outside, Walking,* and other publications. He is the author of two other books, *New England Hiking* (Foghorn Press, 3rd edition, 2002), and *The Ultimate Guide to Backcountry Travel* (AMC Books, 1999). An avid hiker and backpacker, climber, backcountry and Nordic skier, and cyclist, he has hiked extensively in the western United States as well as New England.

Lanza serves as president of the Boise Climbers Alliance and as southern Idaho's volunteer regional coordinator for The Access Fund. During the mid-1990s he wrote a weekly column about New England outdoor activities, which was syndicated in about twenty daily newspapers throughout the region. He also co-hosted a call-in show about the outdoors on New Hampshire Public Radio. Prior to that, he worked as a newspaper reporter and editor in New England. A native of Leominster, Massachusetts, Lanza now lives with his wife, Penny Beach, and their son, Nate, in Boise, Idaho.

The author, Michael Lanza, hiking with his then 11-month-old son, Nate, in August 2000 on the Iceline Trail in Yoho National Park, Canada

THE MOUNTAINEERS, founded in 1906, is a nonprofit outdoor activity and conservation club, whose mission is "to explore, study, preserve, and enjoy the natural beauty of the outdoors . . . . " Based in Seattle, Washington, the club is now the third-largest such organization in the United States, with 15,000 members and five branches throughout Washington State.

The Mountaineers sponsors both classes and year-round outdoor activities in the Pacific Northwest, which include hiking, mountain climbing, ski-touring, snowshoeing, bicycling, camping, kayaking and canoeing, nature study, sailing, and adventure travel. The club's conservation division supports environmental causes through educational activities, sponsoring legislation, and presenting informational programs. All club activities are led by skilled, experienced volunteers, who are dedicated to promoting safe and responsible enjoyment and preservation of the outdoors.

If you would like to participate in these organized outdoor activities or the club's programs, consider a membership in The Mountaineers. For information and an application, write or call The Mountaineers, Club Headquarters, 300 Third Avenue West, Seattle, WA 98119; 206-284-6310.

The Mountaineers Books, an active, nonprofit publishing program of the club, produces guidebooks, instructional texts, historical works, natural history guides, and works on environmental conservation. All books produced by The Mountaineers Books fulfill the club's mission.

Send or call for our catalog of more than 500 outdoor titles:

The Mountaineers Books
1001 SW Klickitat Way, Suite 201
Seattle, WA 98134
800-553-4453
mbooks@mountaineersbooks.org
www.mountaineersbooks.org

The Mountaineers Books is proud to be a corporate sponsor of Leave No Trace, whose mission is to promote and inspire responsible outdoor recreation through education, research, and partnerships. The Leave No Trace program is focused specifically on human-powered (nonmotorized) recreation.

Leave No Trace strives to educate visitors about the nature of their recreational impacts, as well as offer techniques to prevent and minimize such impacts. Leave No Trace is best understood as an educational and ethical program, not as a set of rules and regulations.

For more information, visit *www.LNT.org,* or call 800-332-4100.

Other titles you might enjoy from The Mountaineers Books

Available at fine bookstores and outdoor stores, by phone at 800-553-4453, or on the web at *www.mountaineersbooks.org*

Everyday Wisdom: 1001 Expert Tips for Hikers by Karen Berger. $16.95 paperbound. 0-89886-523-9.

More Everyday Wisdom: Trail-Tested Advice from the Experts by Karen Berger. $16.95 paperbound. 0-89886-899-8.

Backcountry Cooking: From Pack to Plate in 10 Minutes by Dorcas Miller. $16.95 paperbound. 0-89886-551-4.

More Backcountry Cooking: Moveable Feasts by the Experts by Dorcas Miller. $16.95 paperbound. 0-89886-900-5.

Wilderness 911: A Step-by-Step Guide for Medical Emergencies and Improvised Care in the Backcountry by Eric A. Weiss, M.D. $16.95 paperbound. 0-89886-597-2.

Making Camp: A Complete Guide for Hikers, Mountain Bikers, Paddlers & Skiers by Steve Howe, Alan Kesselheim, Dennis Coello, and John Harlin. $16.95 paperbound. 0-89886-522-0.

Leave No Trace: A Guide to the New Wilderness Etiquette, 2nd Edition by Annette McGivney. $11.95 paperbound. 0-89886-910-2.

Don't Get Sick: The Hidden Dangers of Camping and Hiking by Buck Tilton, M.S., and Rick Bennett, Ph.D. $6.95 paperbound. 0-89886-854-8.

Staying Found: The Complete Map & Compass Handbook, 3rd Edition by June Fleming. $12.95 paperbound. 0-89886- 785-1.

Wilderness Navigation: Finding Your Way Using Map, Compass, Altimeter, & GPS, 2nd Edition by Mike Burns and Bob Burns. $12.95 paperbound. 0-89886-953-6.

GPS Made Easy: Using Global Positioning Systems in the Outdoors, 4th Edition by Lawrence Letham. $15.95 paperbound. 0-89886-823-8.

Backcountry Bear Basics: The Definitive Guide to Avoiding Unpleasant Encounters by David Smith. $10.95 paperbound. 0-89886-500-X.

Outdoor Leadership: Technique, Common Sense & Self-Confidence by John Graham. $16.95 paperbound. 0-89886-502-6.

Conditioning for Outdoor Fitness: A Comprehensive Training Guide, 2nd Edition by David Musnick, M.D. and Mark Pierce, A.T.C. $24.95 paperbound. 0-89886-756-8.

Photography Outdoors: A Field Guide for Travel & Adventure Photographers, 2nd Edition by Mark Gardner and Art Wolfe. $14.95 paperbound. 0-89886-888-2.